MANY PETTY TORTURES OF SARAH PALIN

MANY PETTY TORTURES OF SARAH PALIN

SNARKY FAT BASTARD

MALEVOLENT BOOKS
Santa Monica, California

MANY PETTY TORTURES OF SARAH PALIN

Copyright © 2011 Snarky Fat Bastard

All Rights Reserved. No part of this book may be used or reproduced in any manner whatsoever without the written permission of the Publisher. This book is a work of fiction. Any references to historical events, real people, or real locales are used fictitiously. Other names, characters, places, and incidents are the product of the author's imagination, and any resemblance to actual events or locales or persons, living or dead, is entirely coincidental.

ISBN: 9781936573028

Published by Malevolent Books
171 Pier Avenue, #328
Santa Monica, California 90405 USA

Email your comments about the book (or don't) to Bastard at snarkyfatbastard@gmail.com. They may or may not get read and may or may not get a reply.

Without limiting the rights under copyright reserved above, no part of this publication may be reproduced, stored in or introduced into a retrieval system, or transmitted, in any form or by any means (electronic, mechanical, photocopying, recording or otherwise), without the prior written permission of both the copyright owner and the above publisher of this book.

For my mom and my dad

MANY PETTY TORTURES OF SARAH PALIN

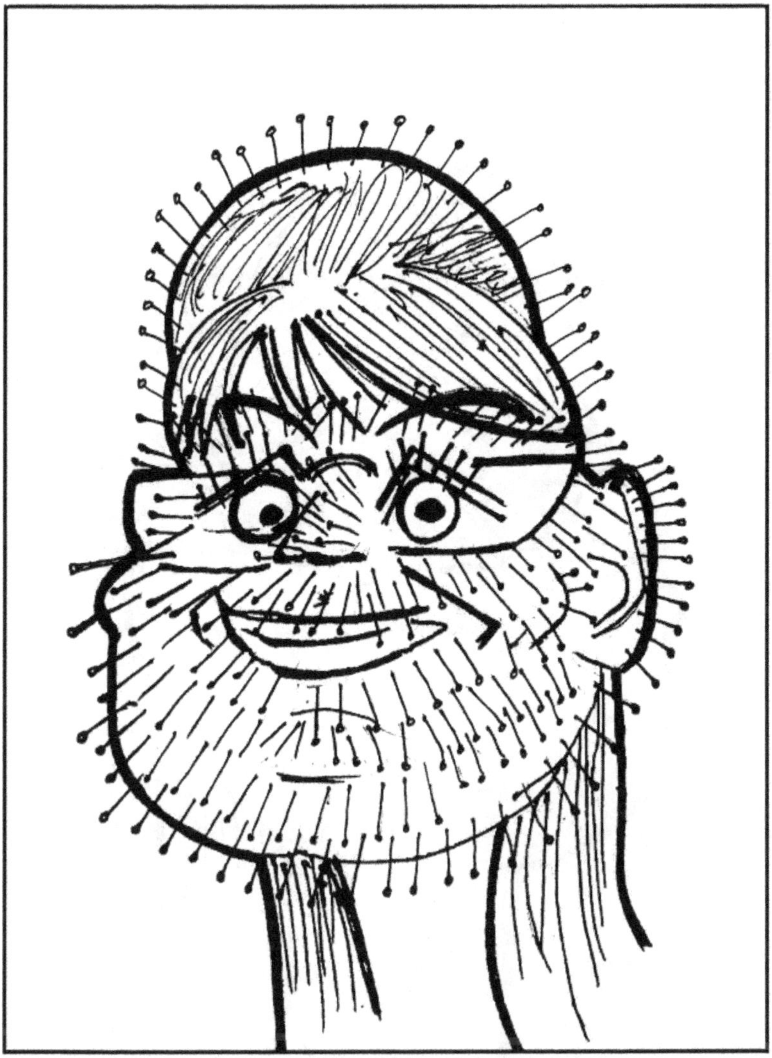

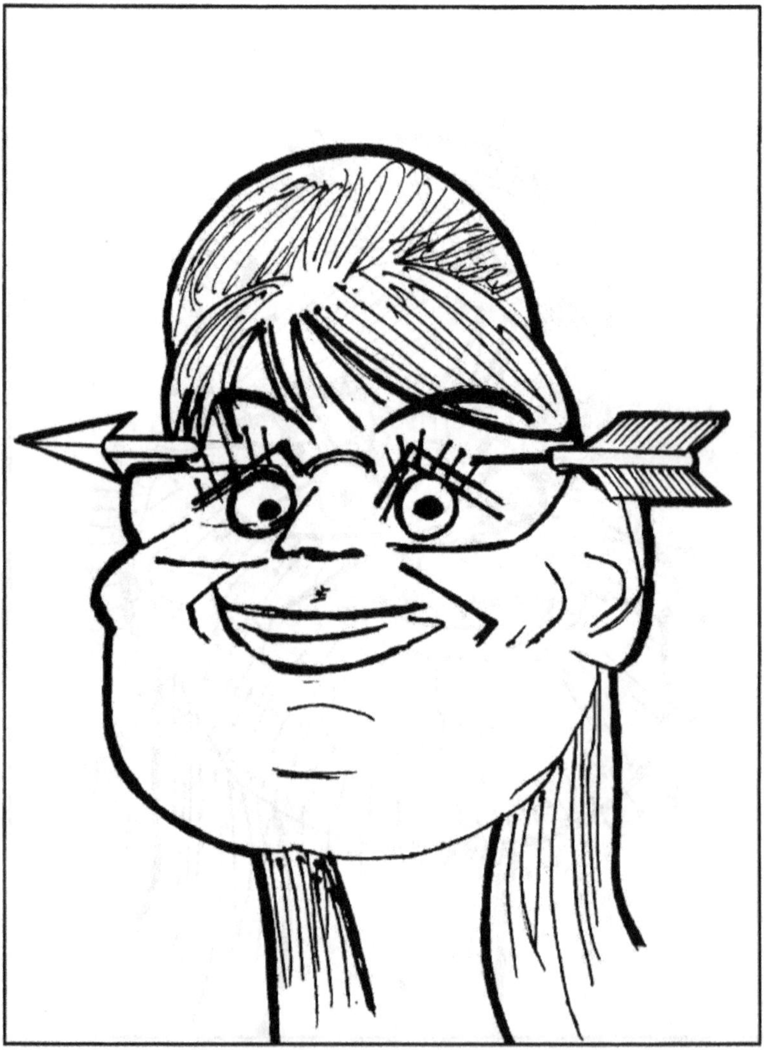

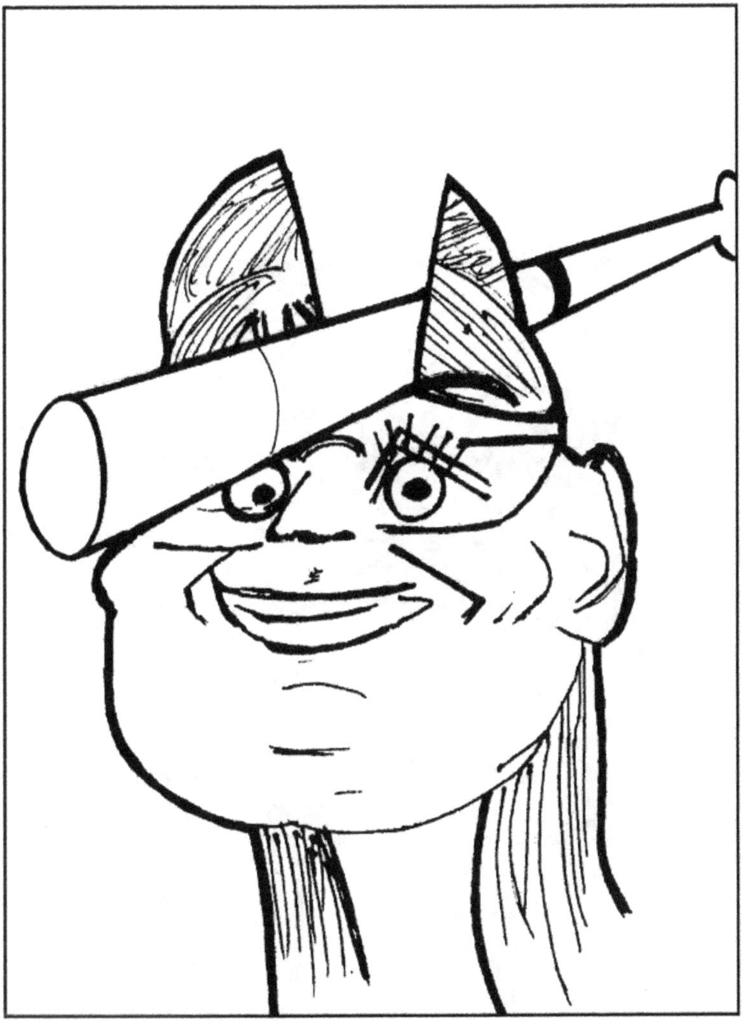

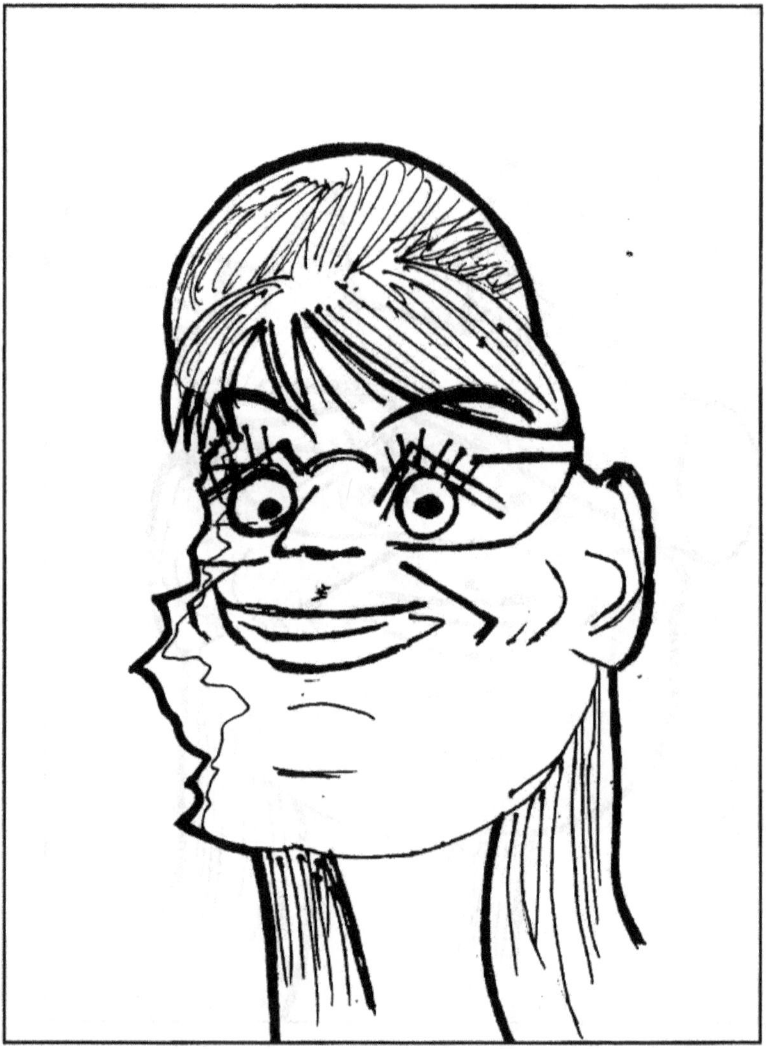

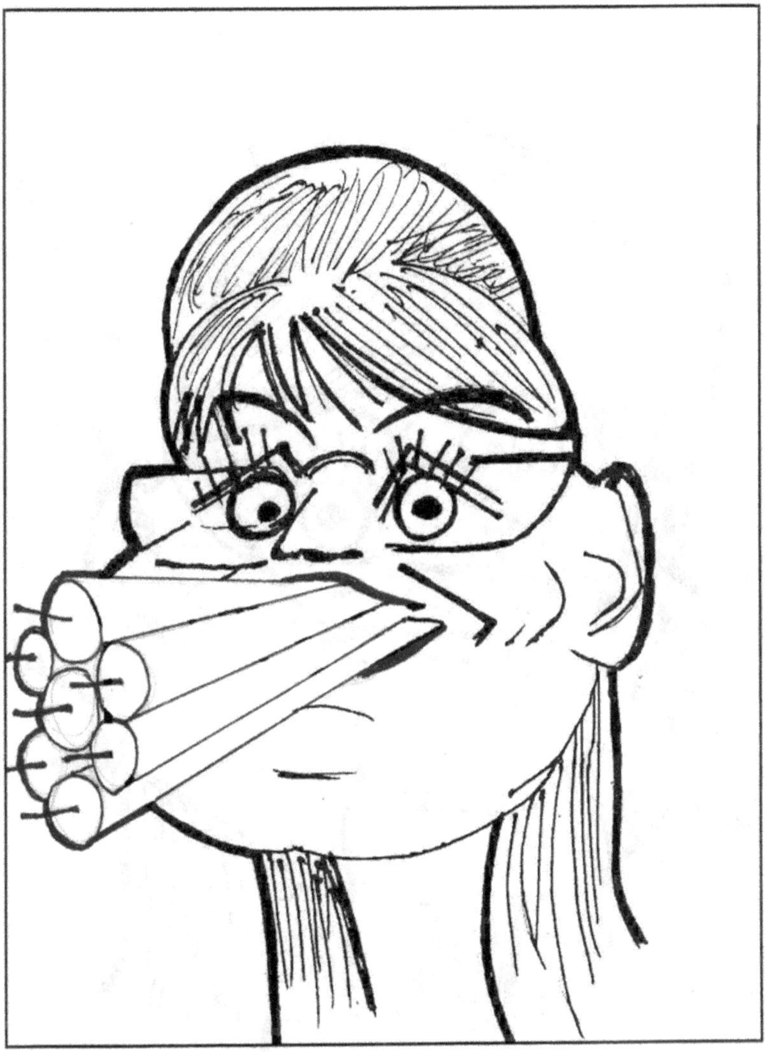

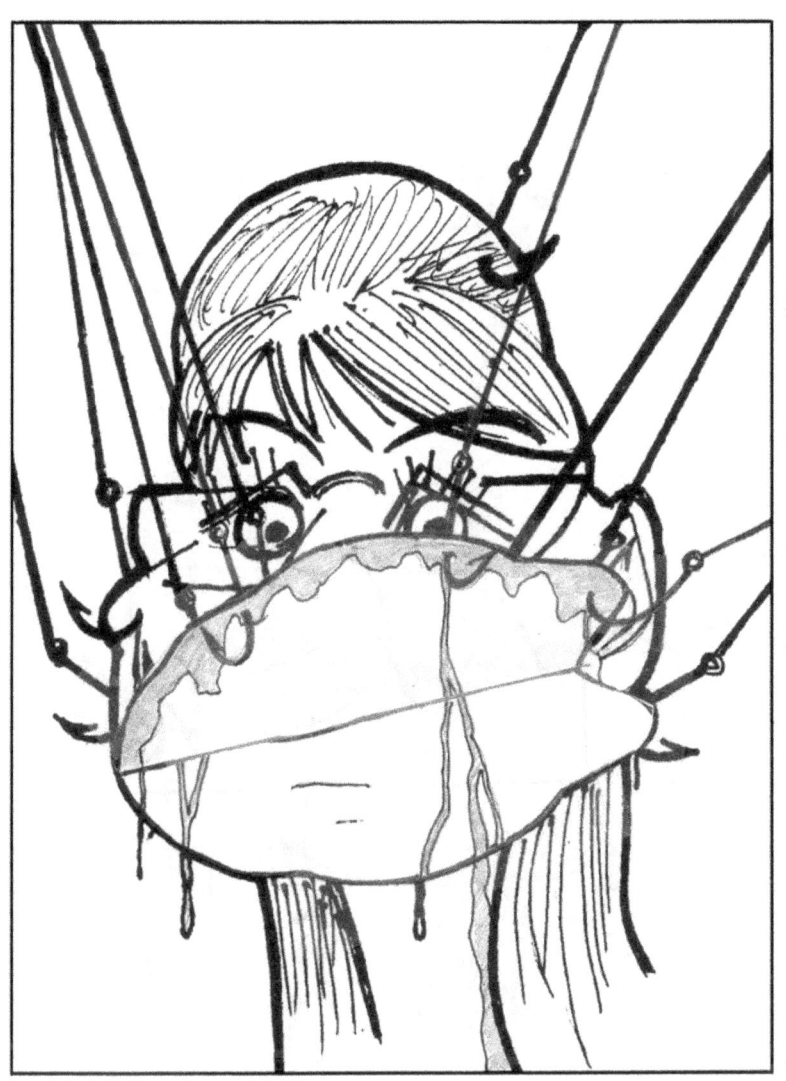

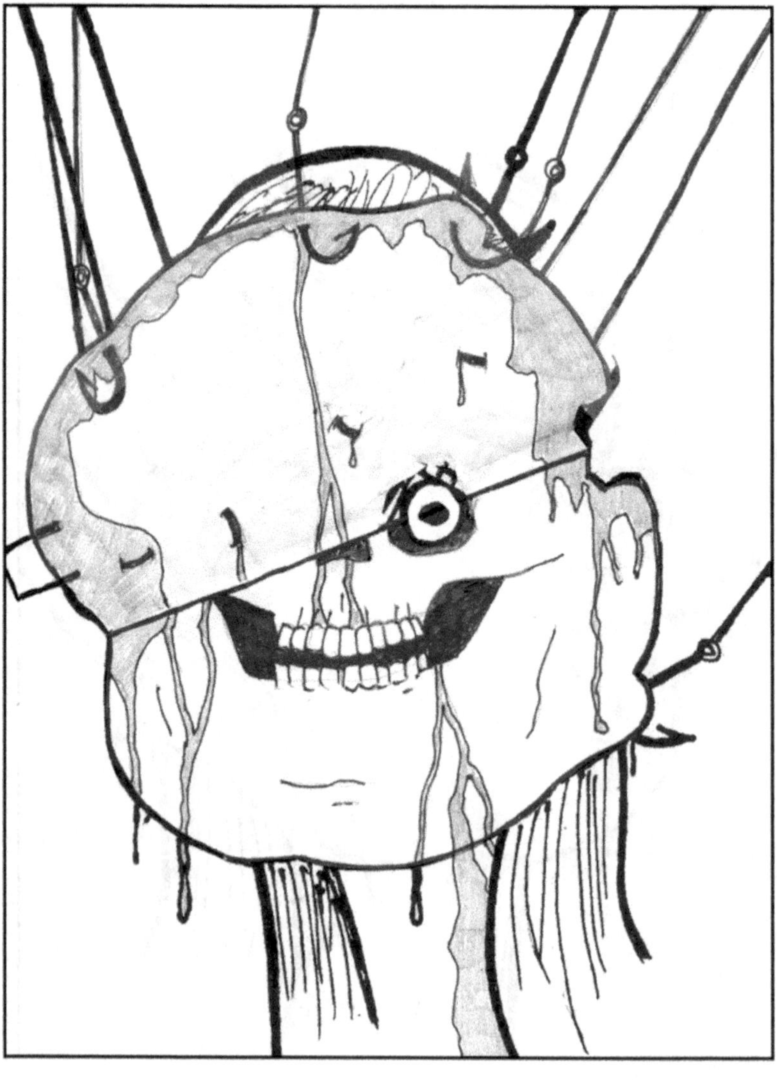

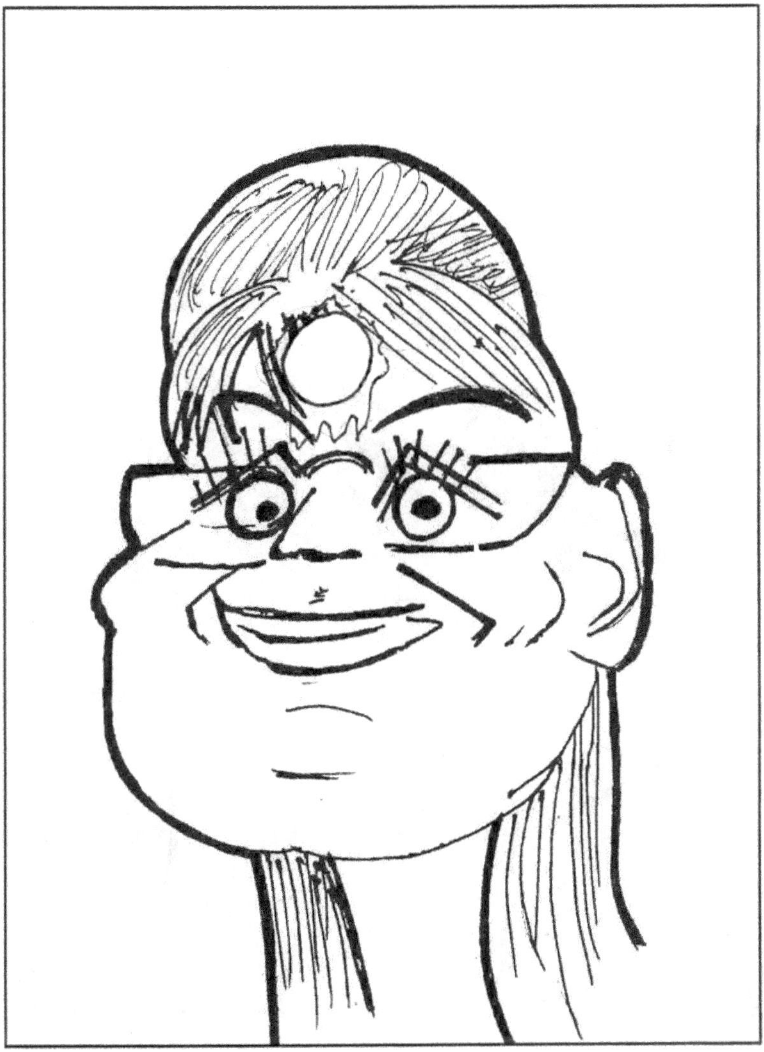

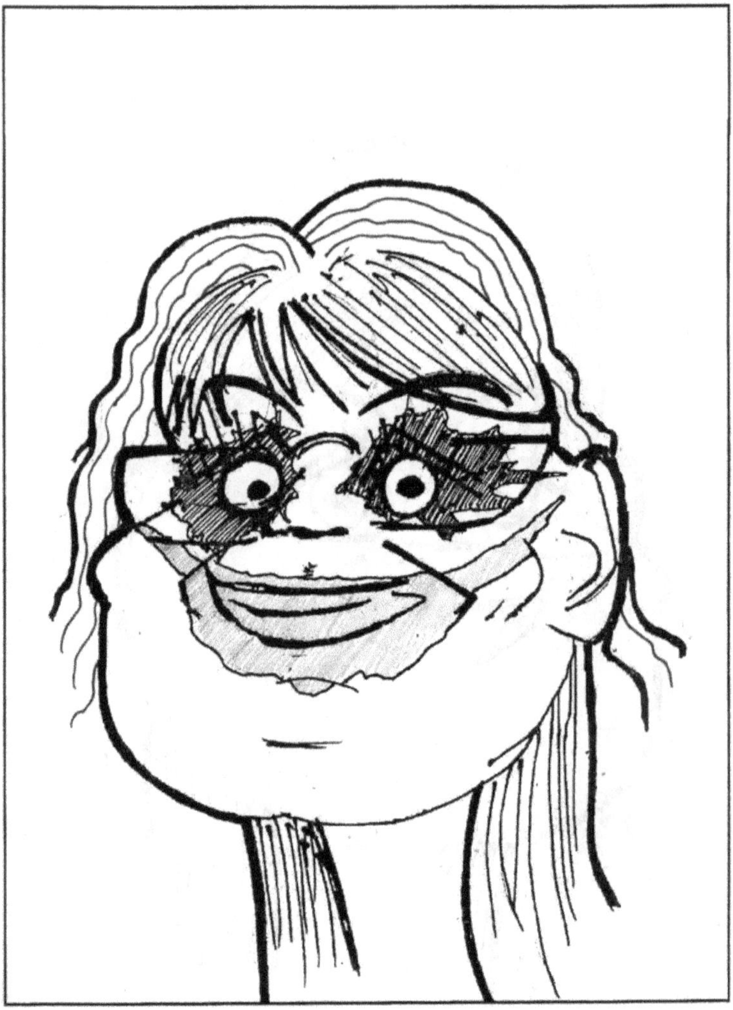

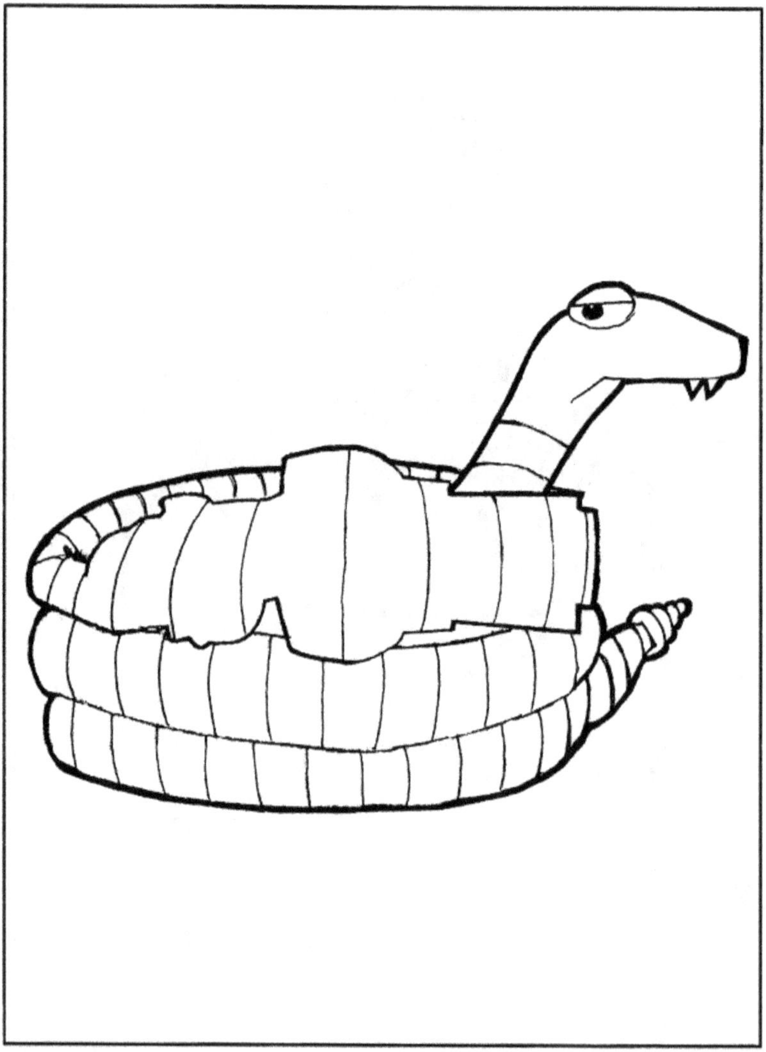

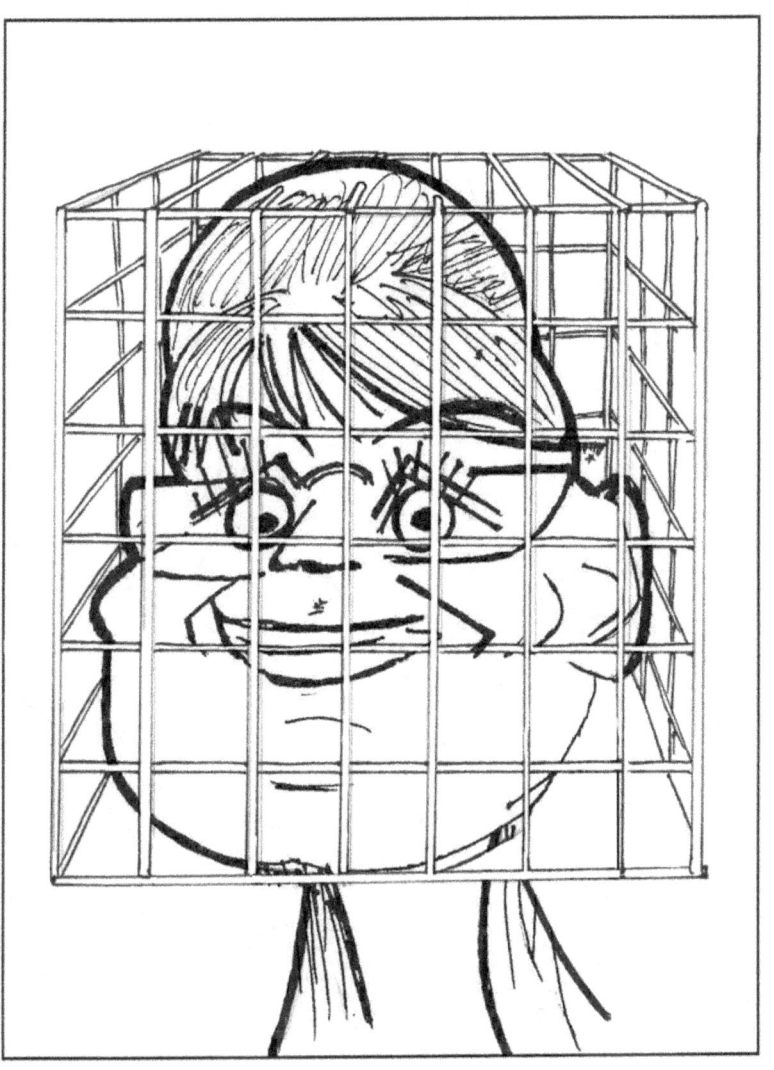

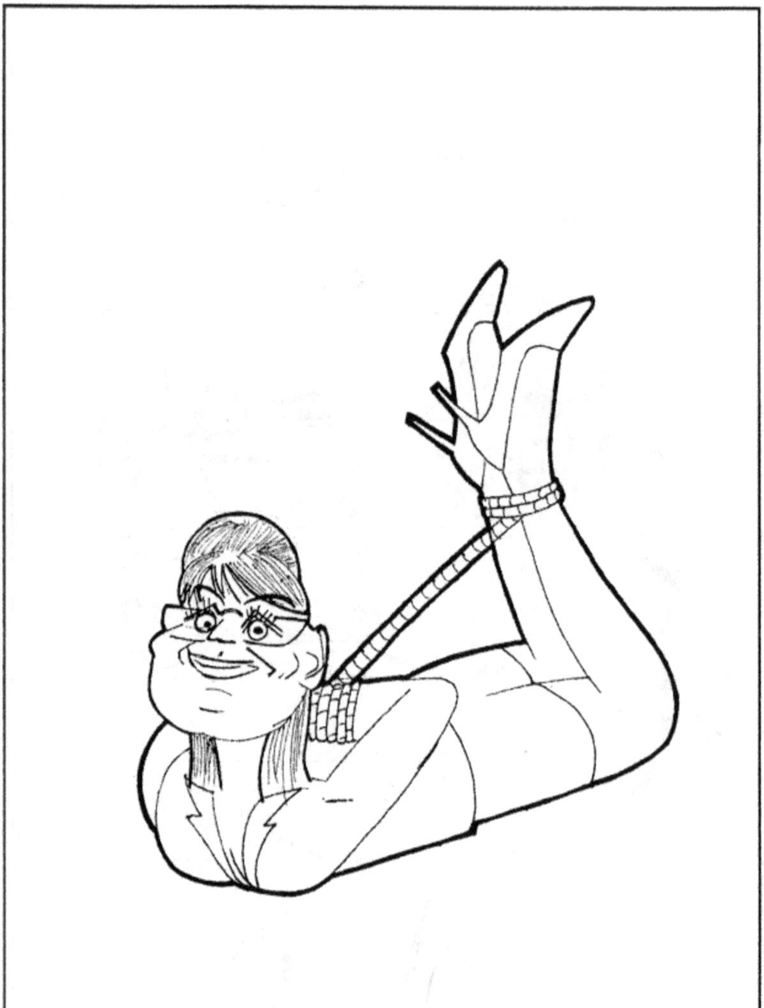

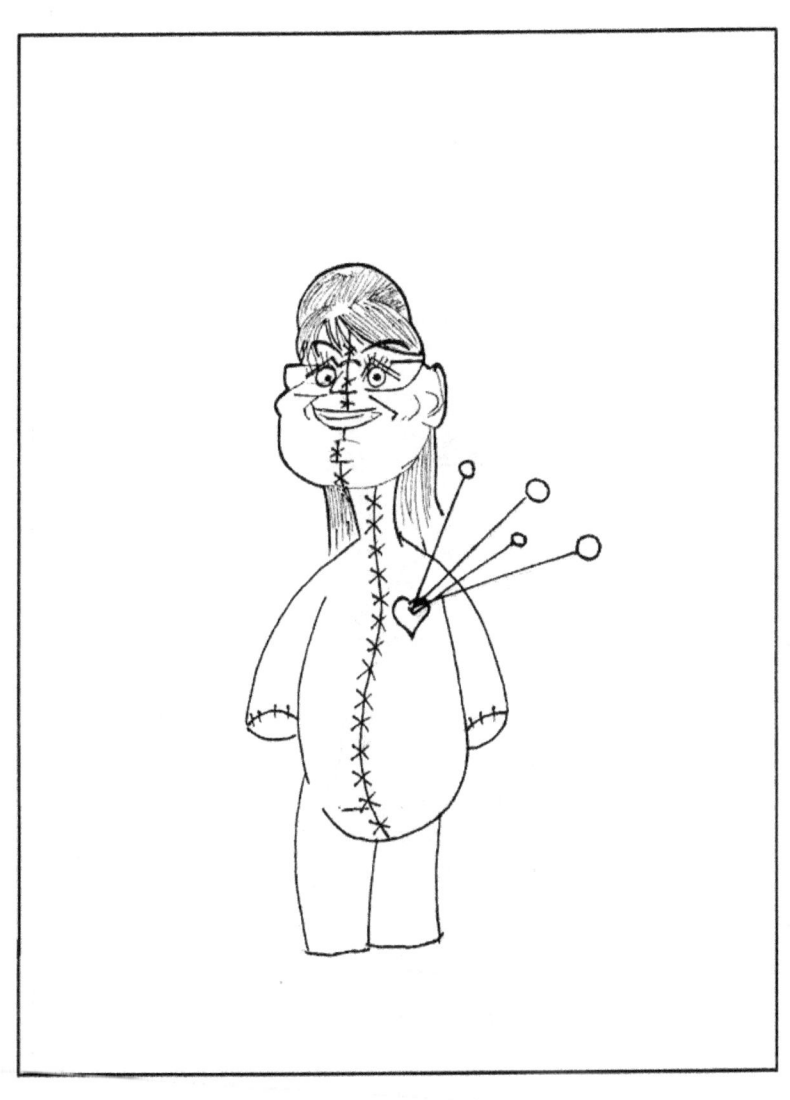

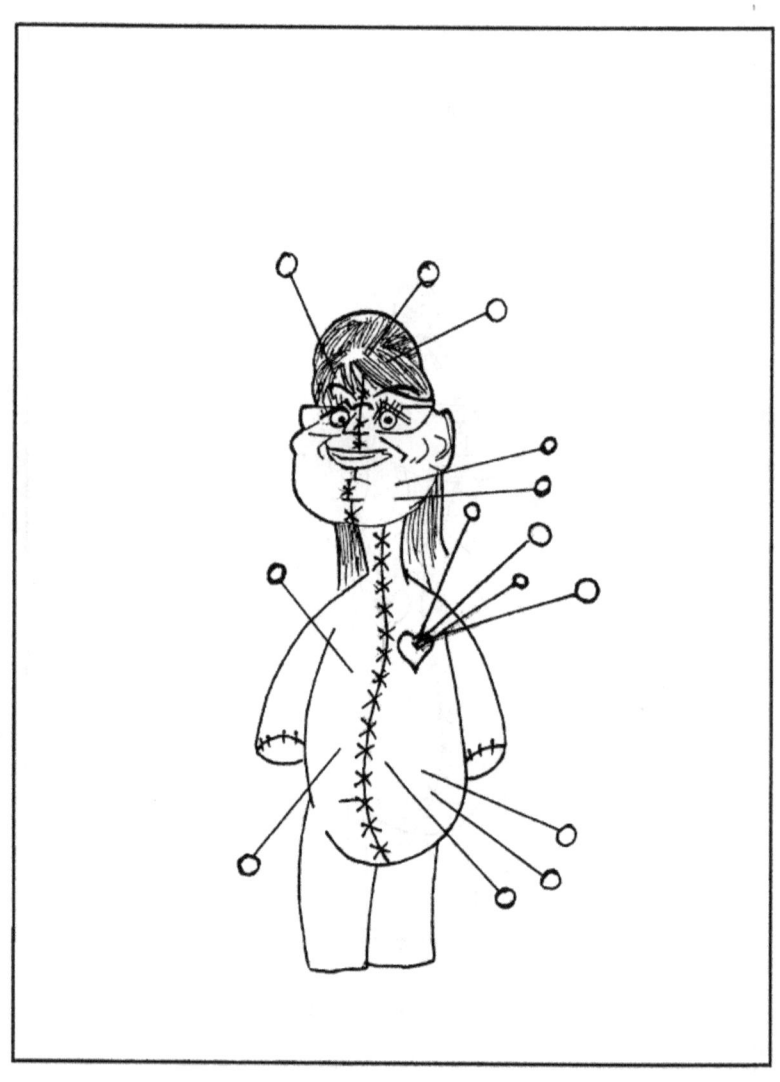

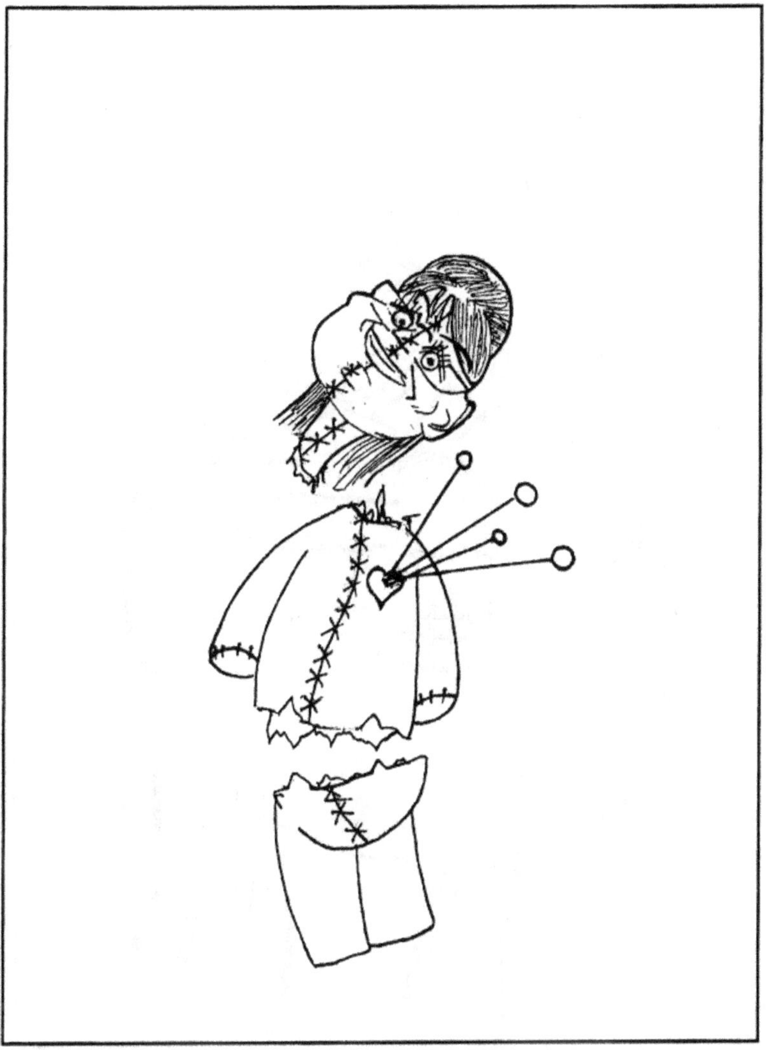

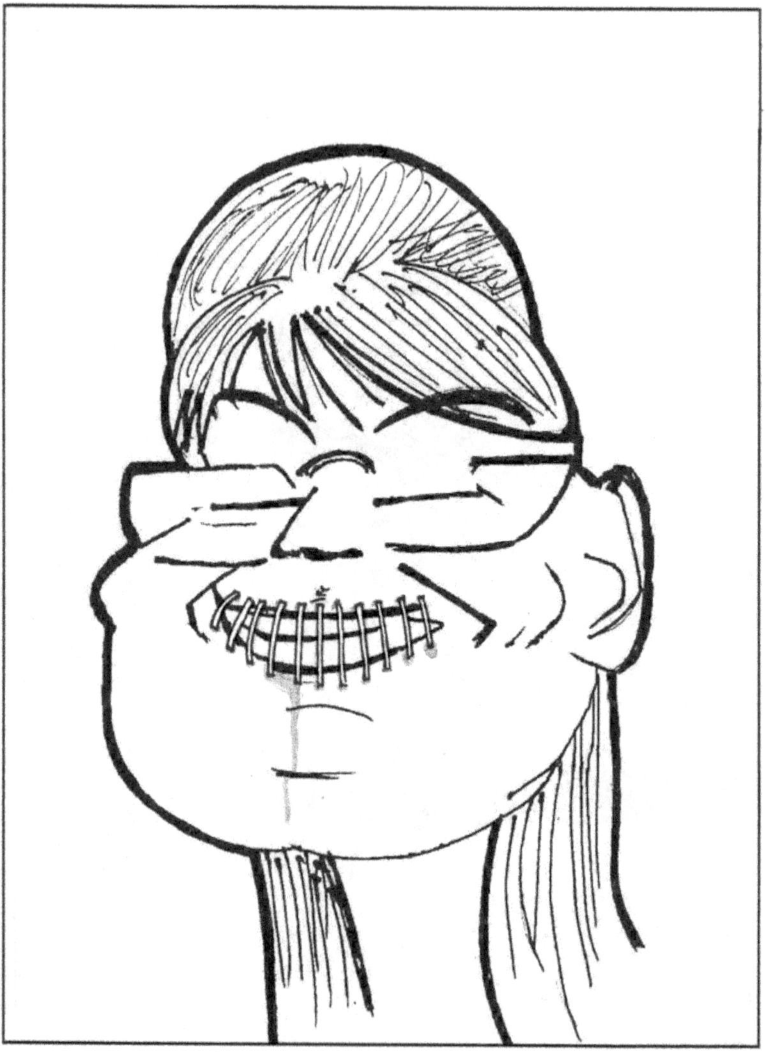

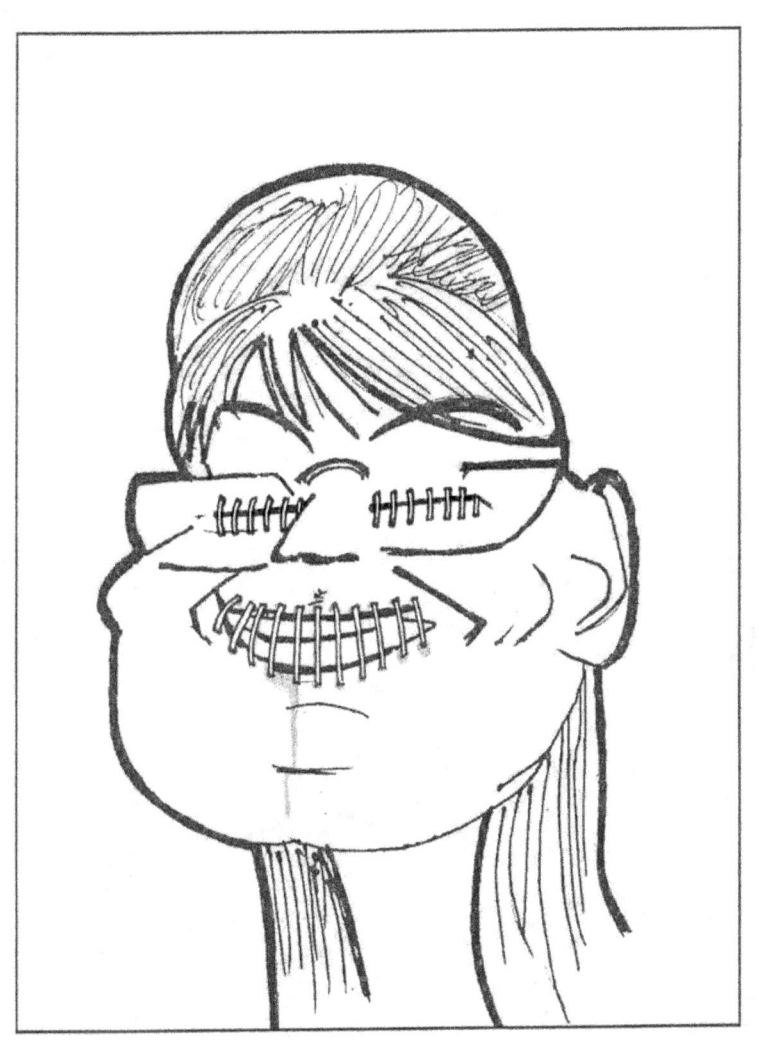

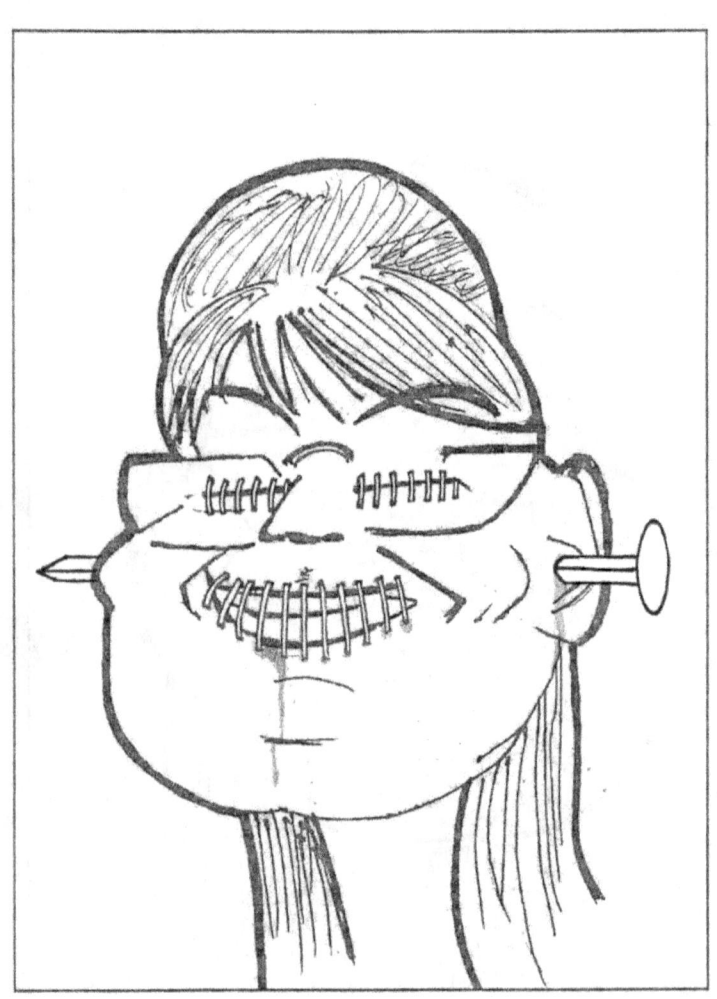

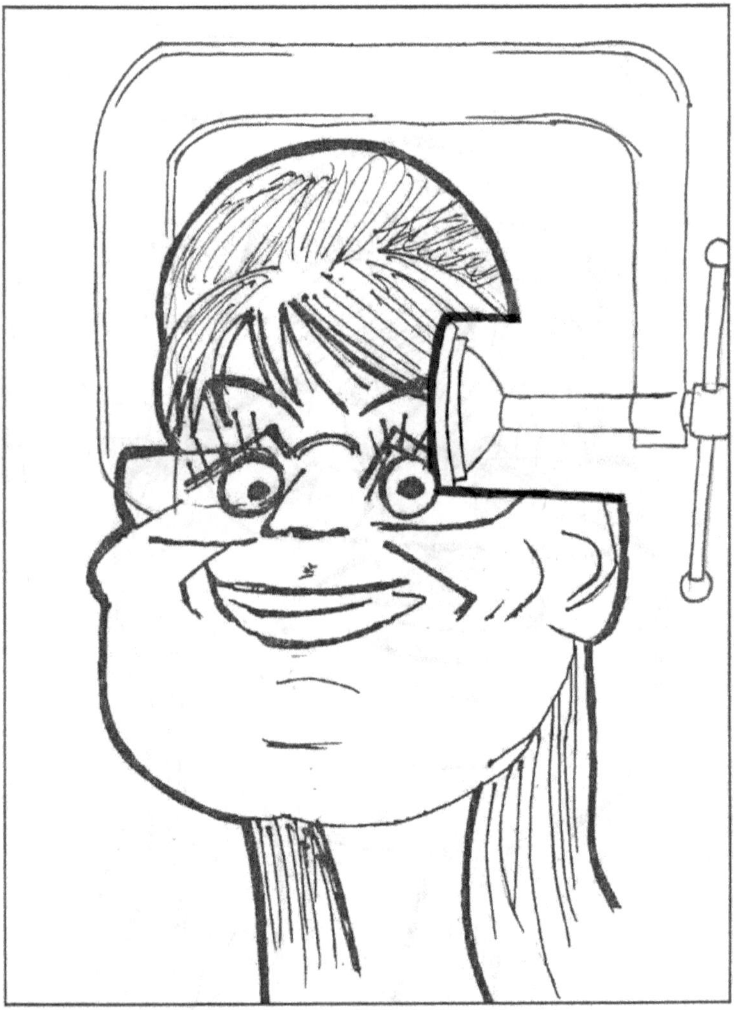

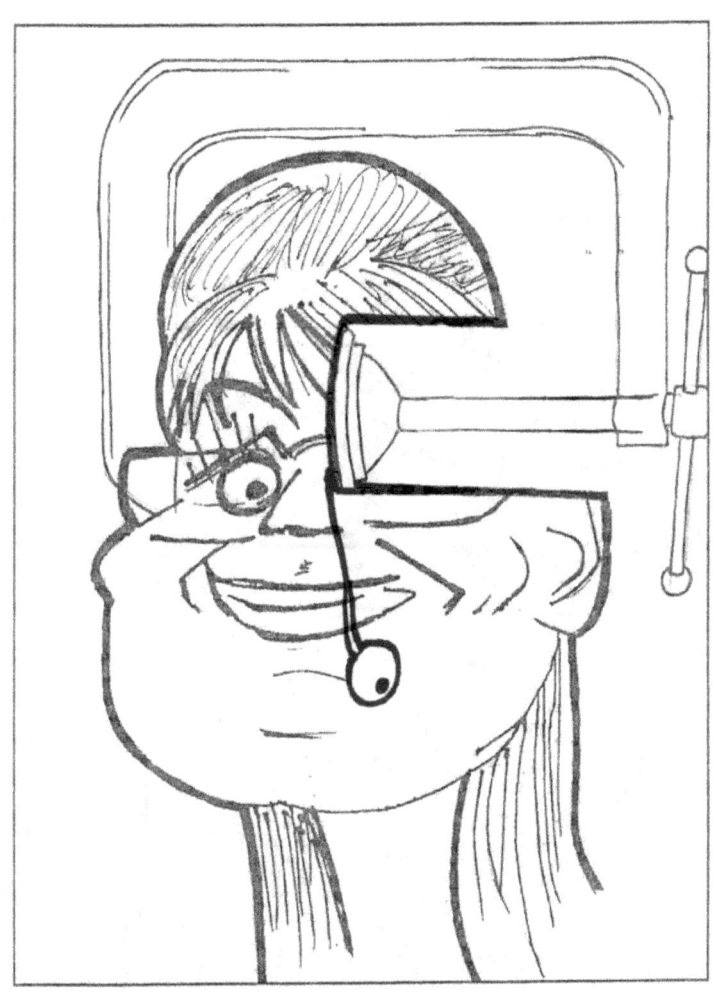

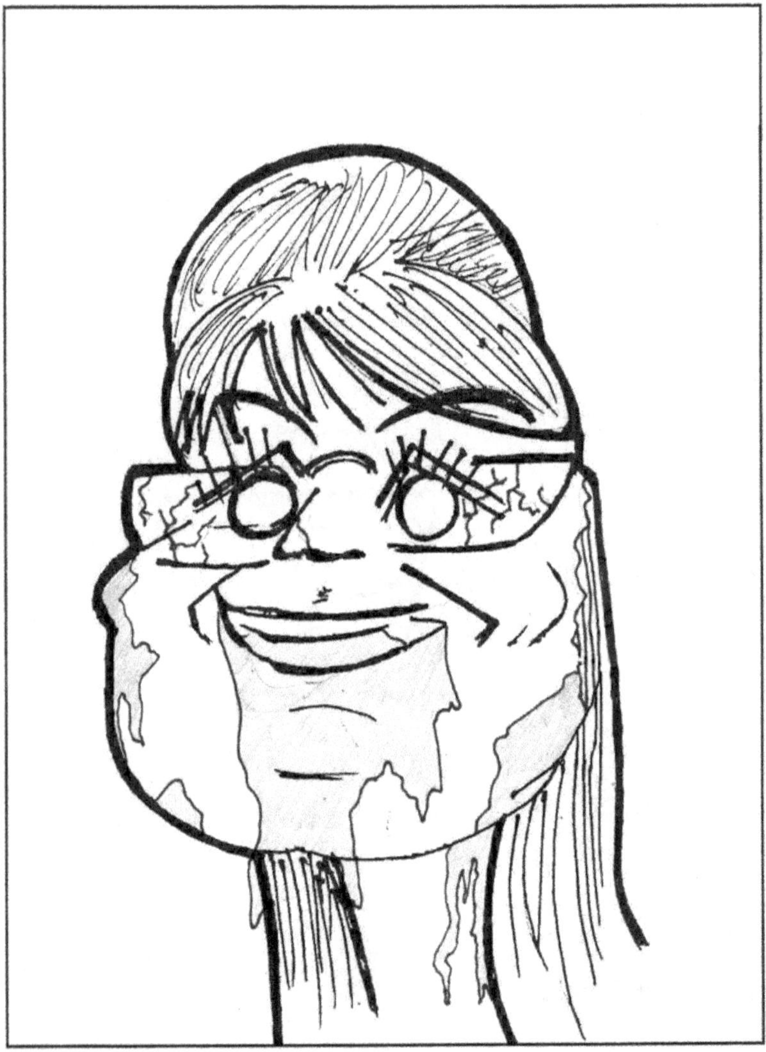

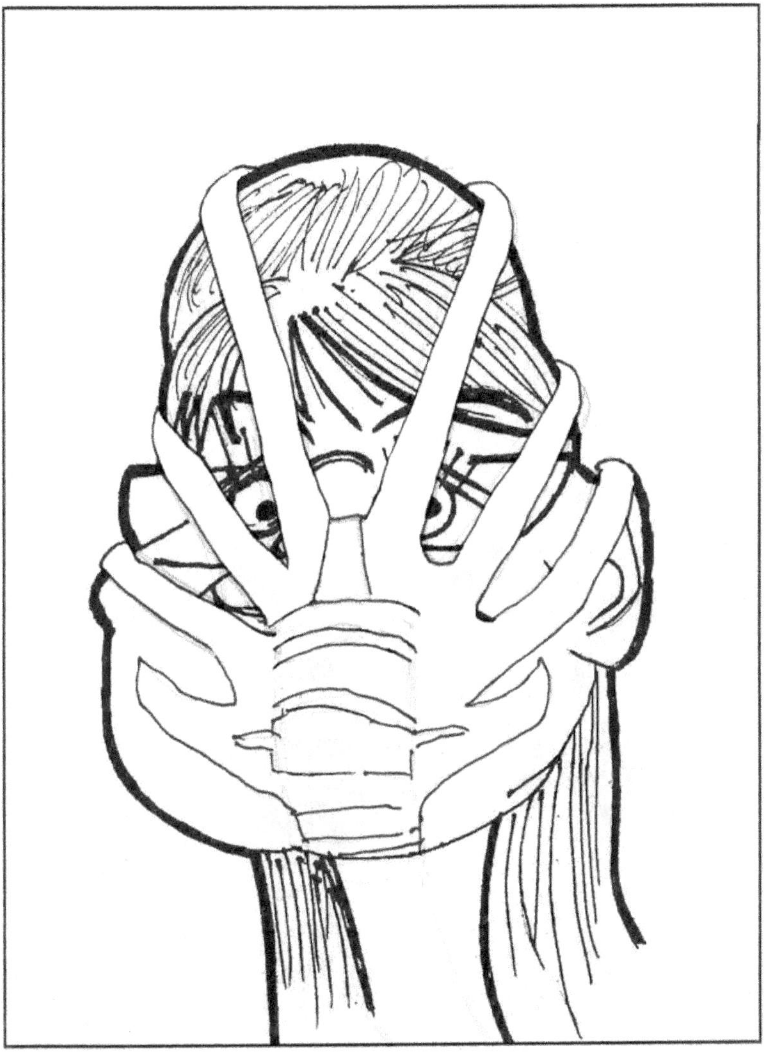

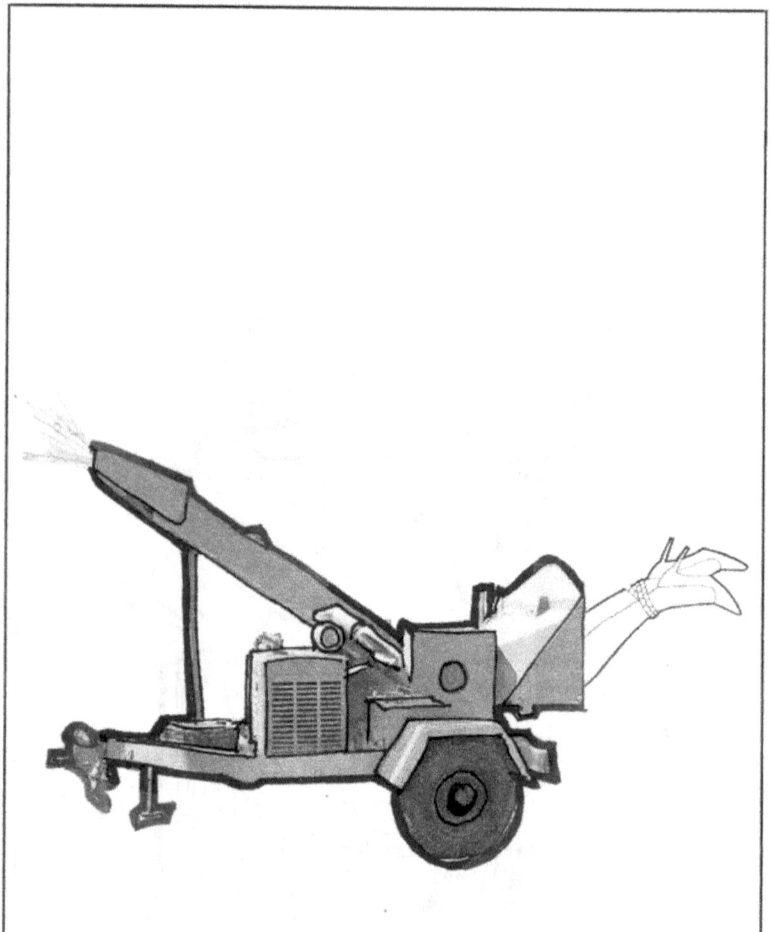

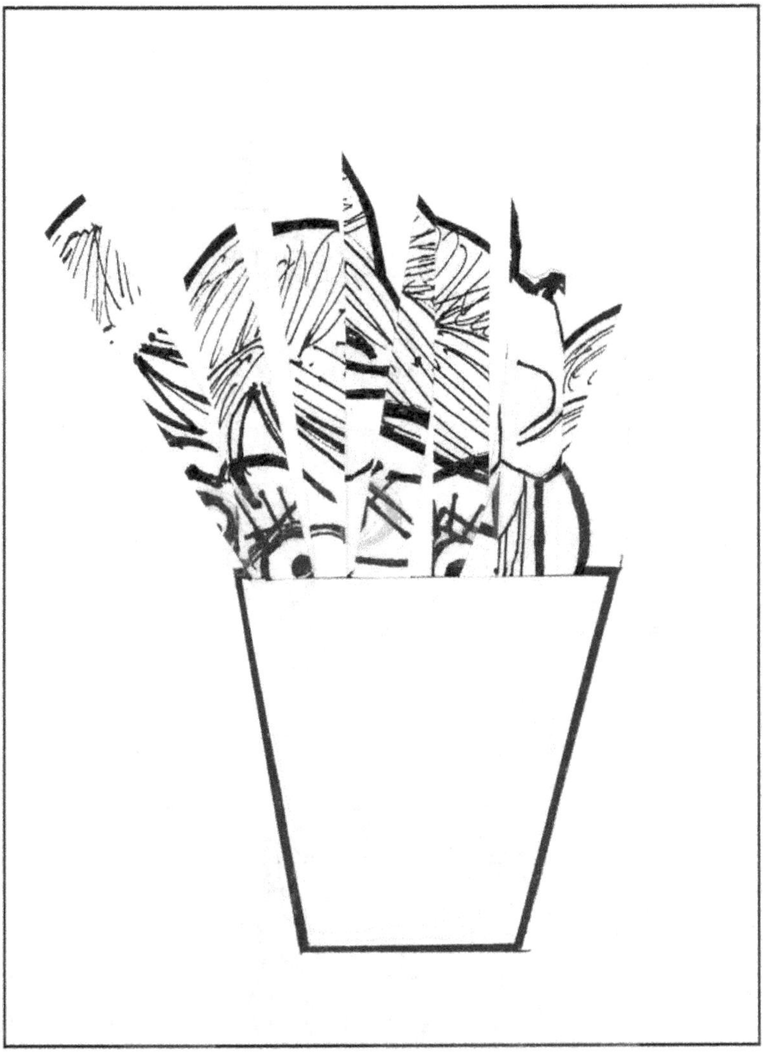

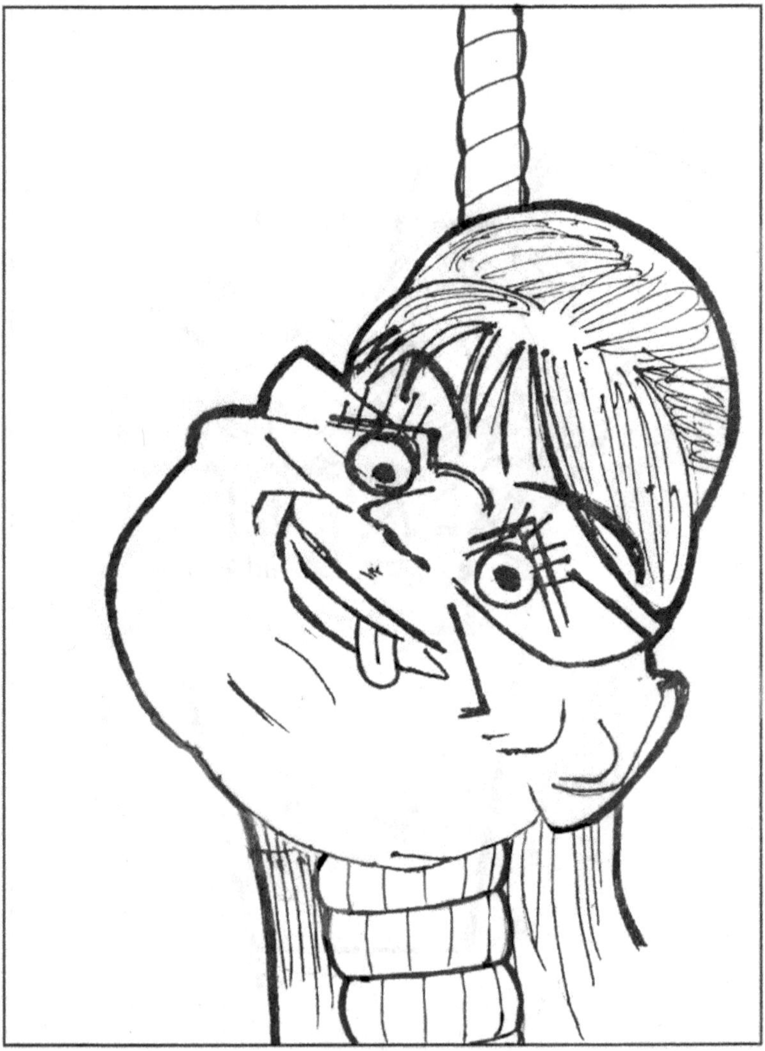

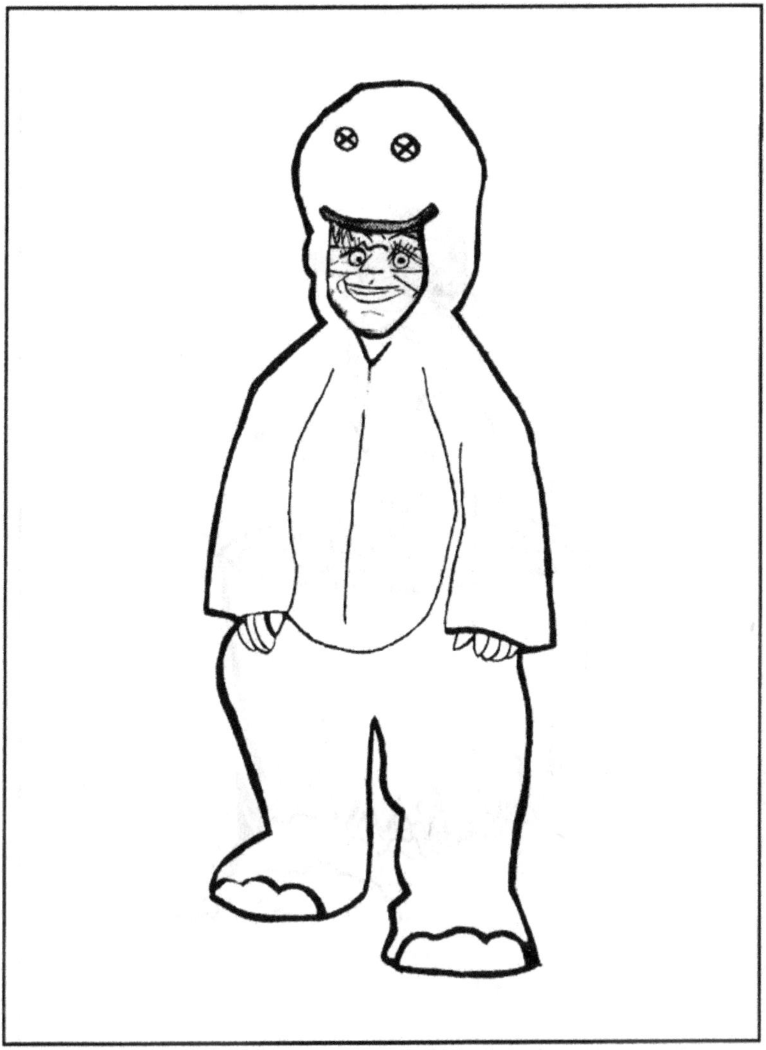

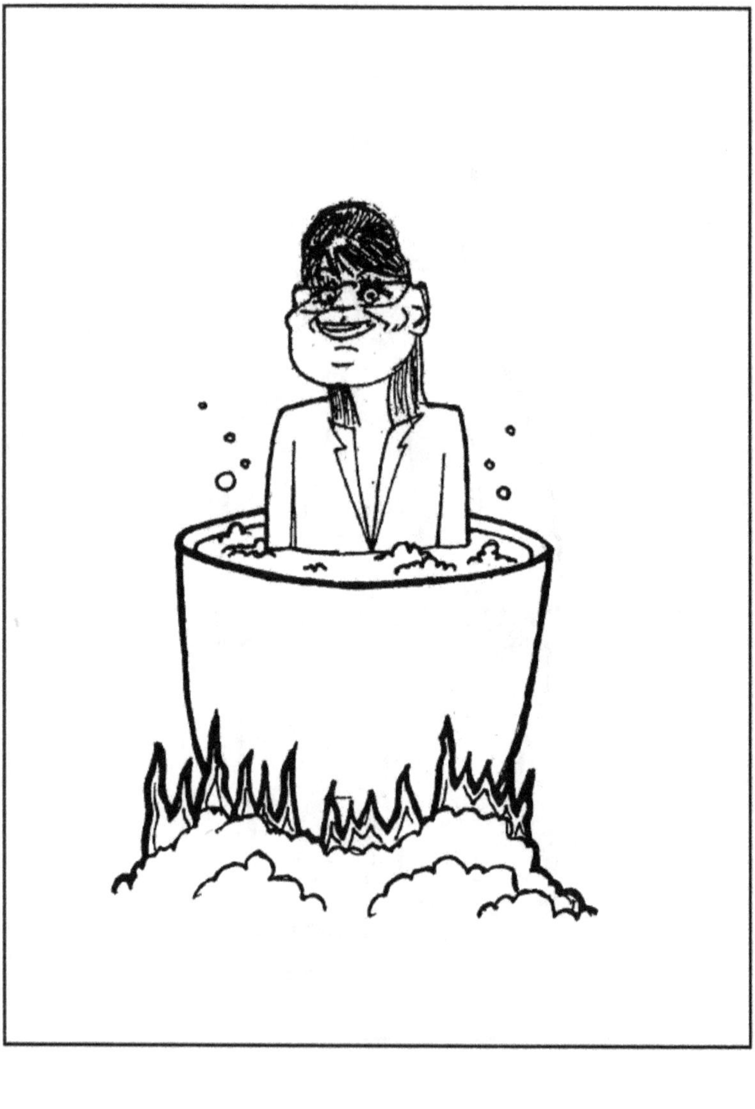

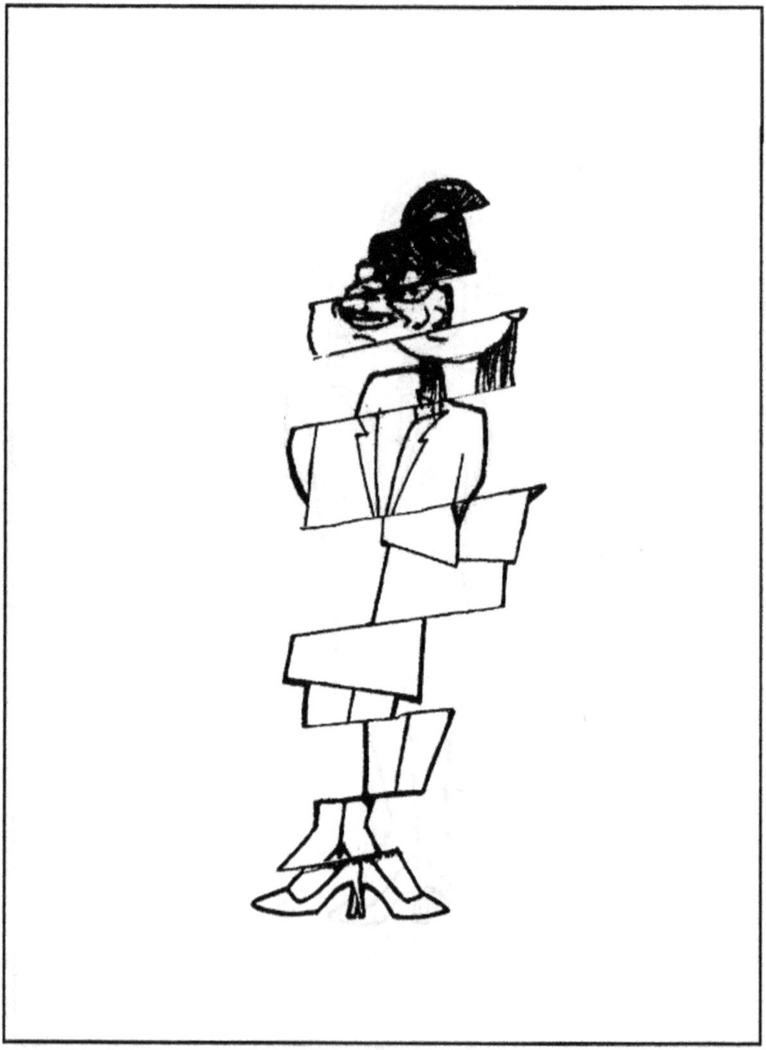

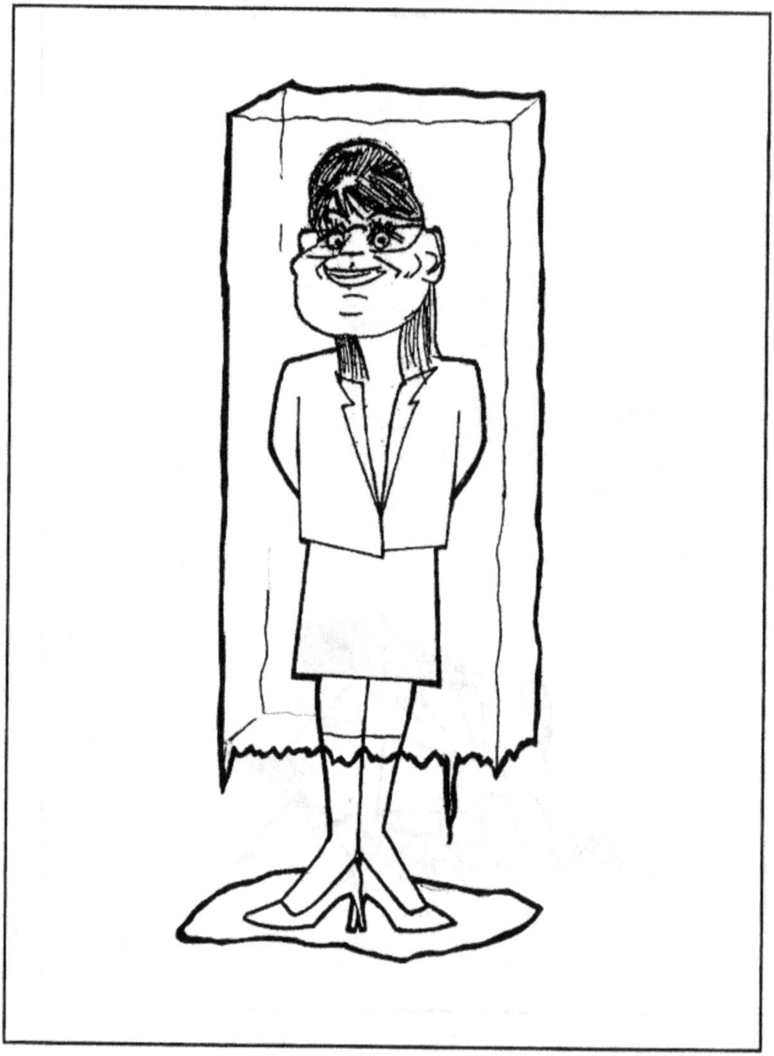

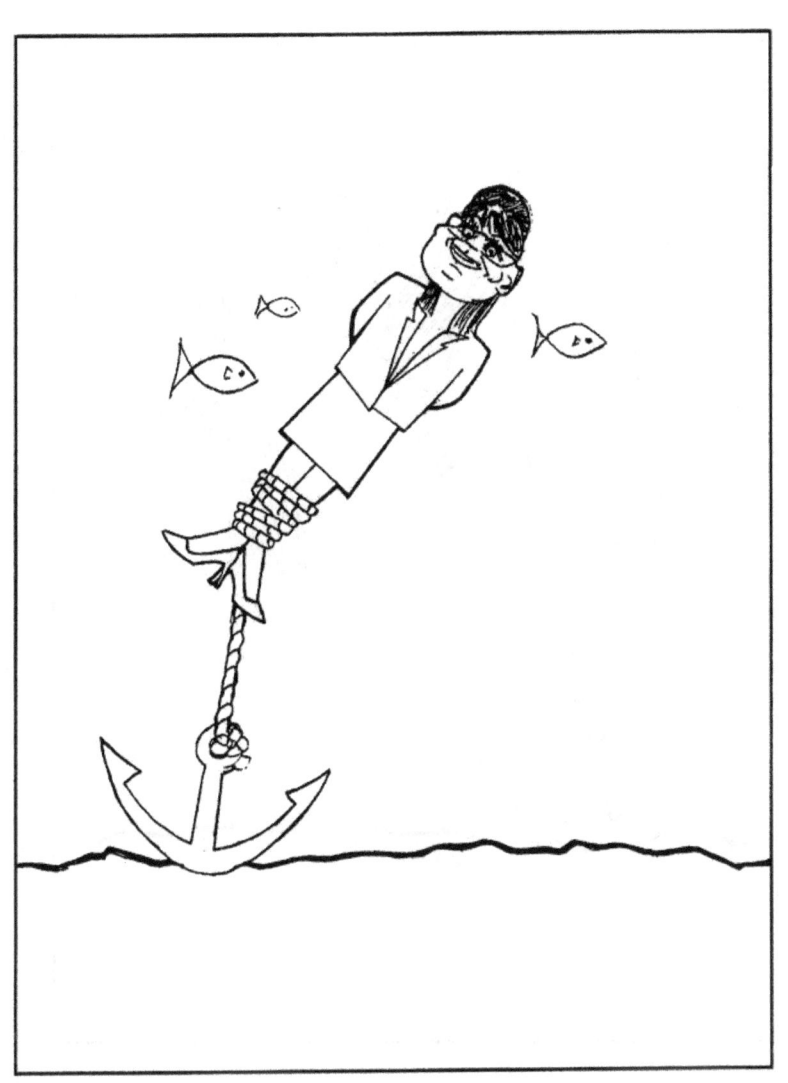

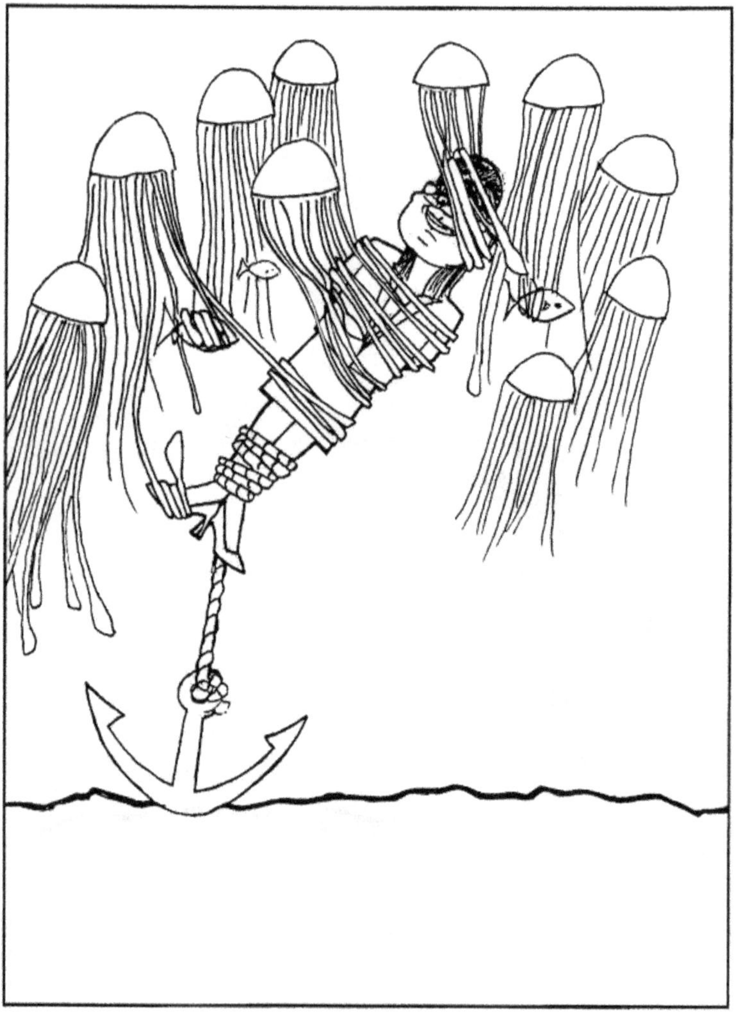

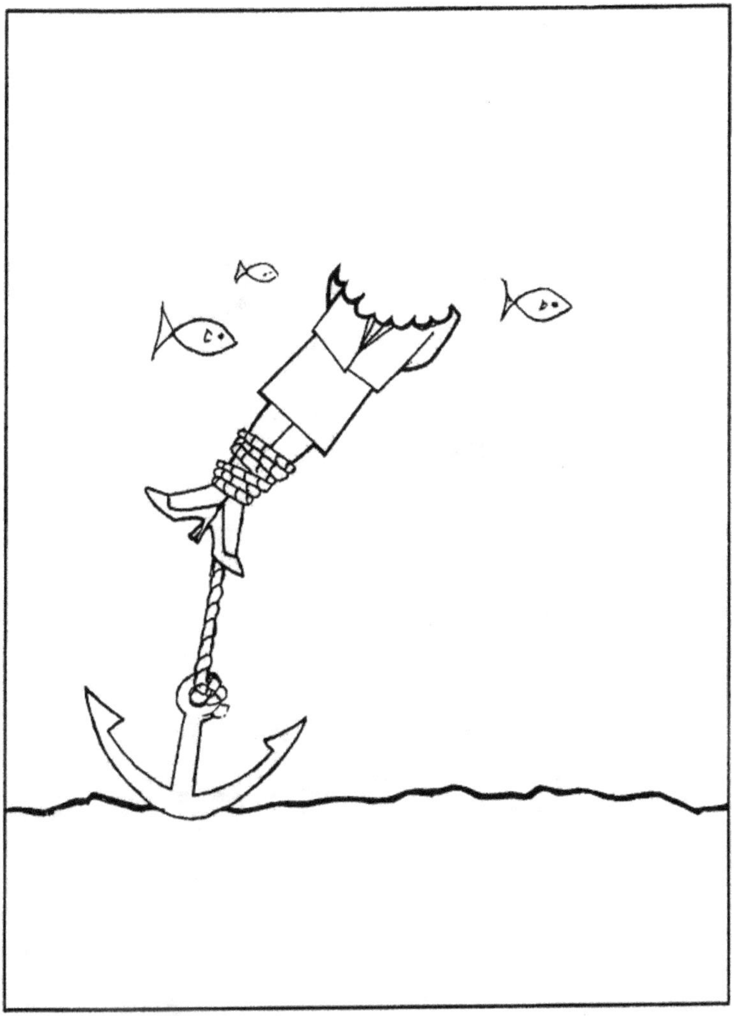

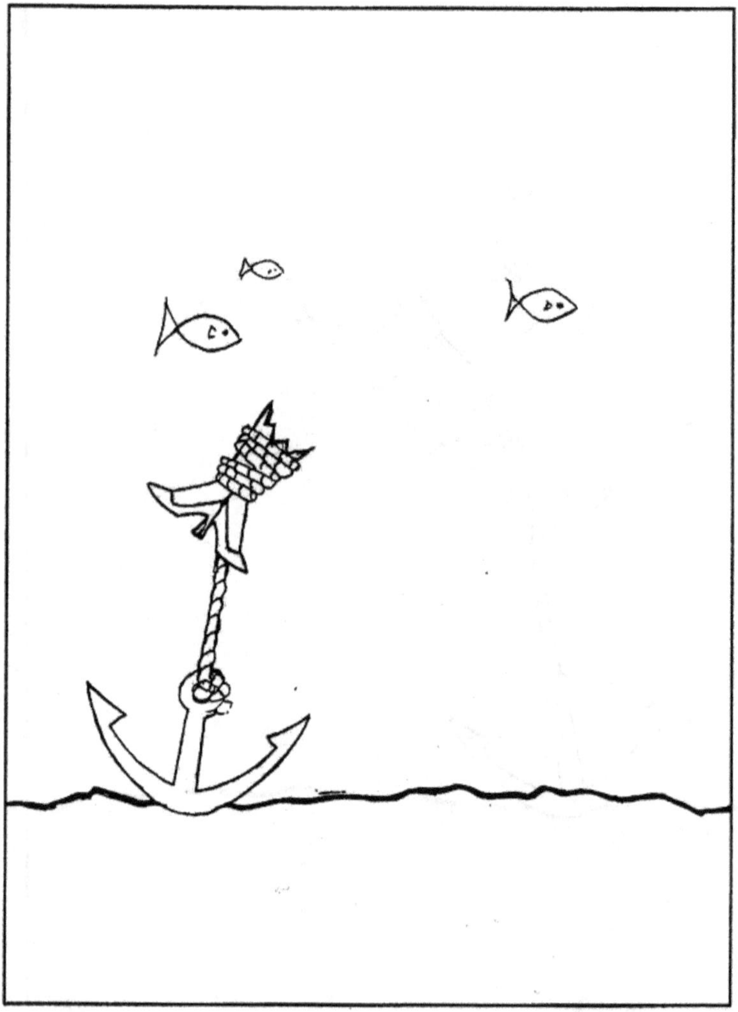

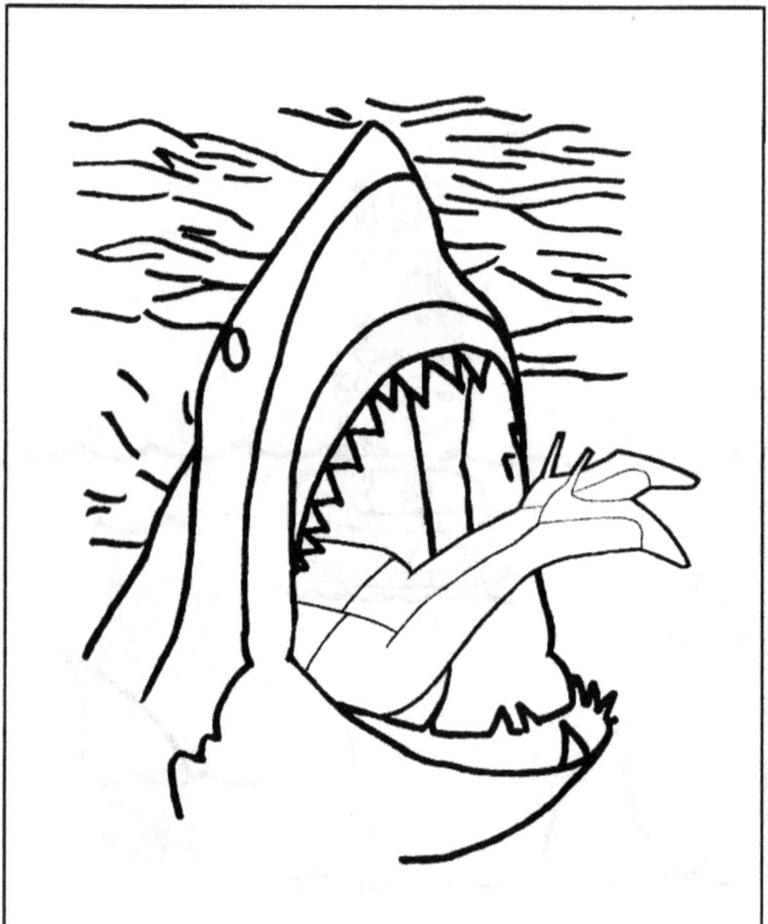

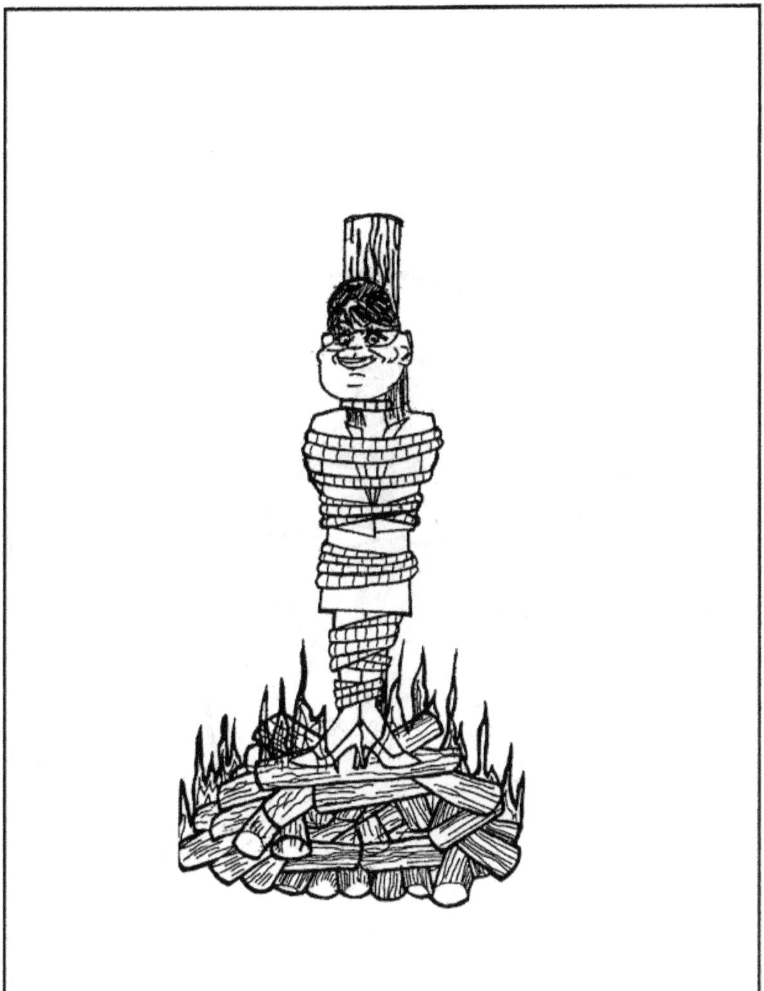

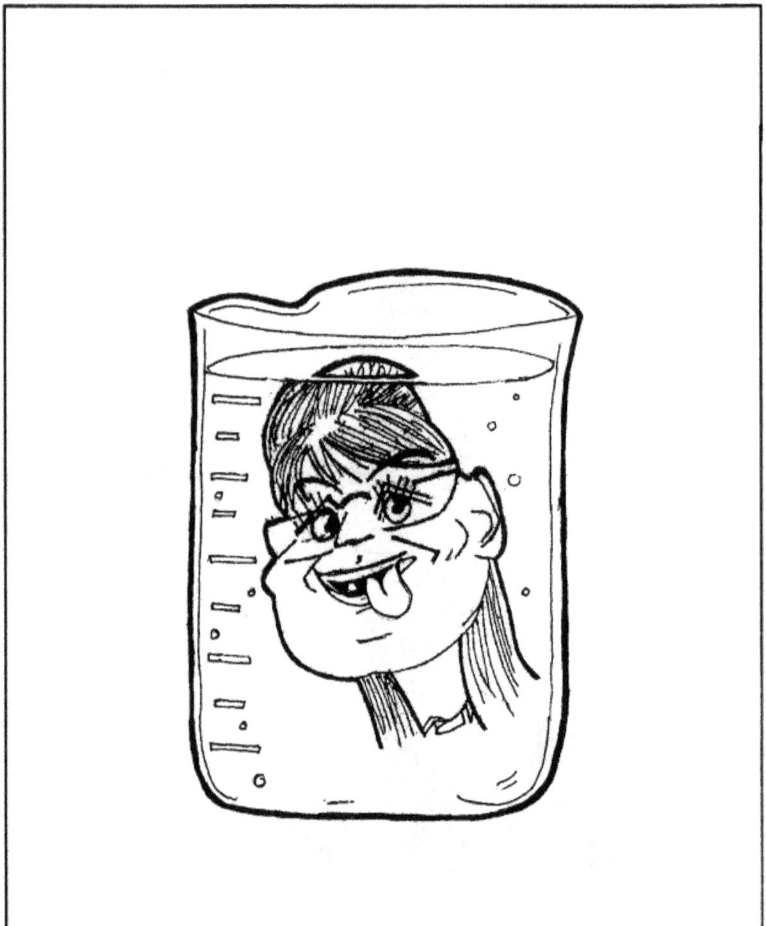

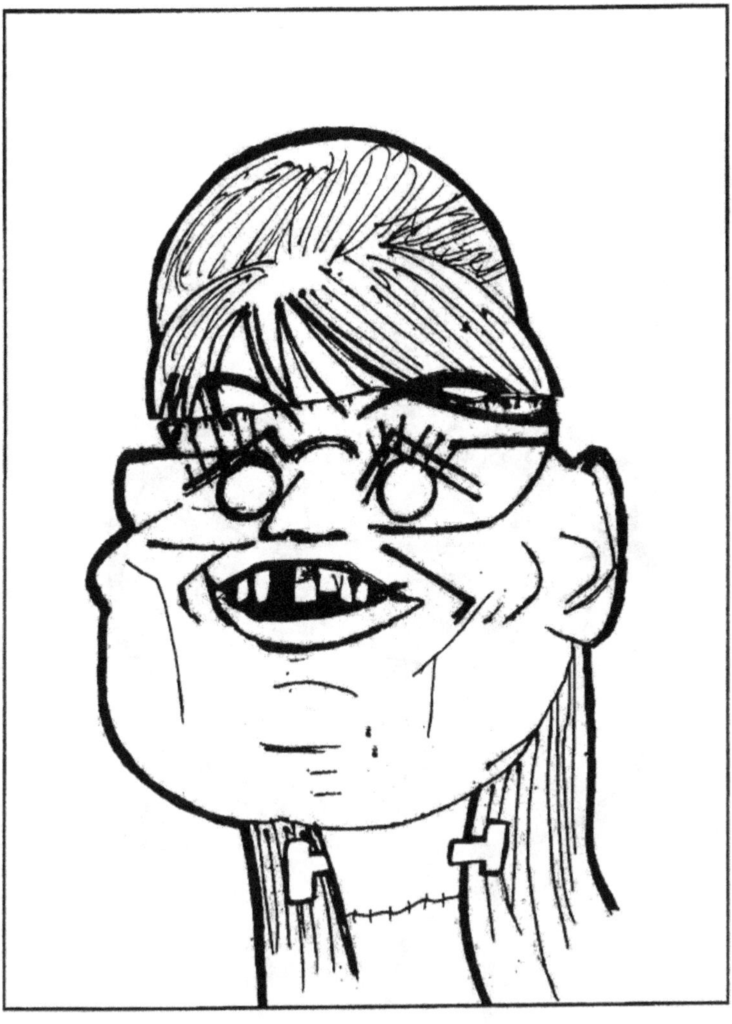

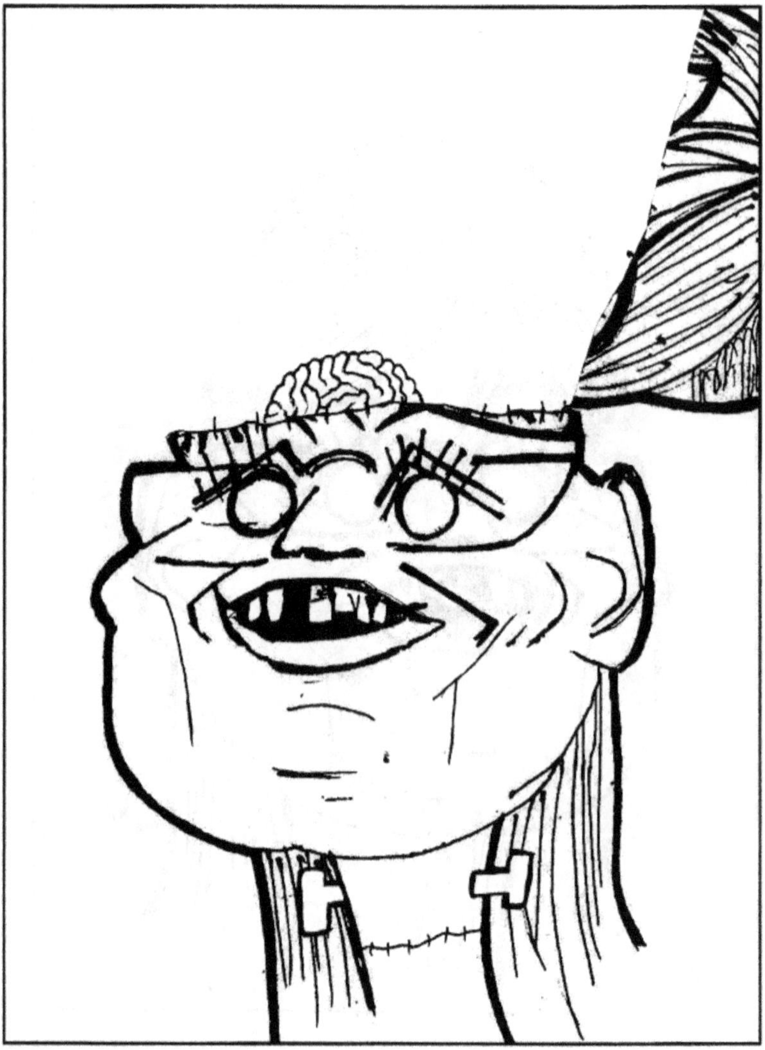

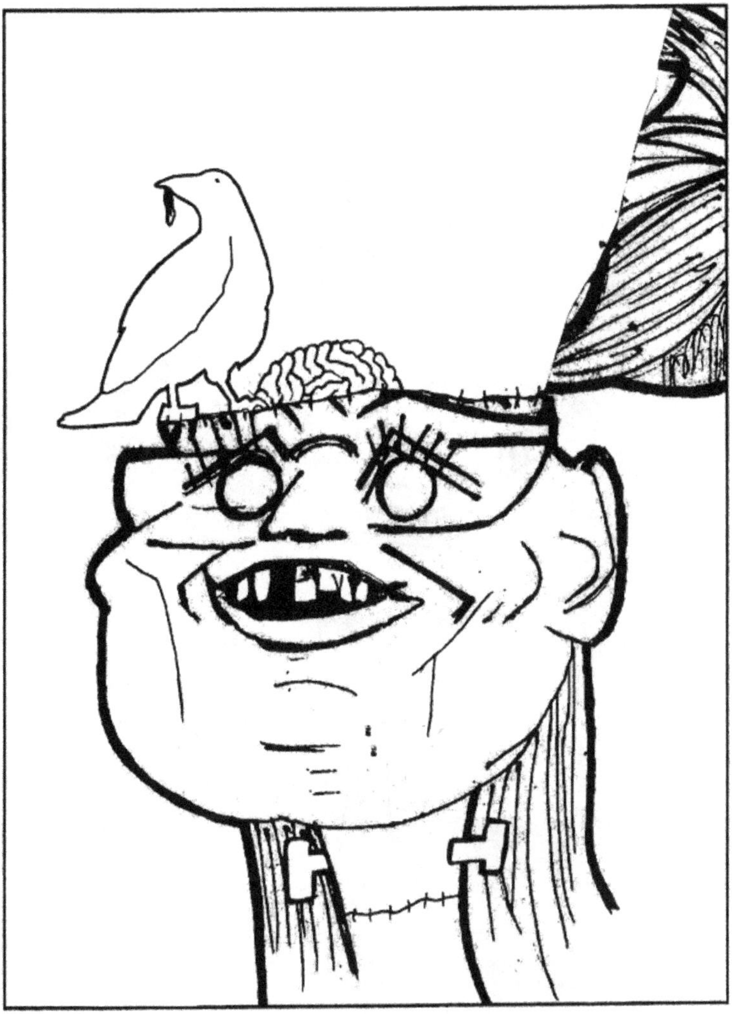

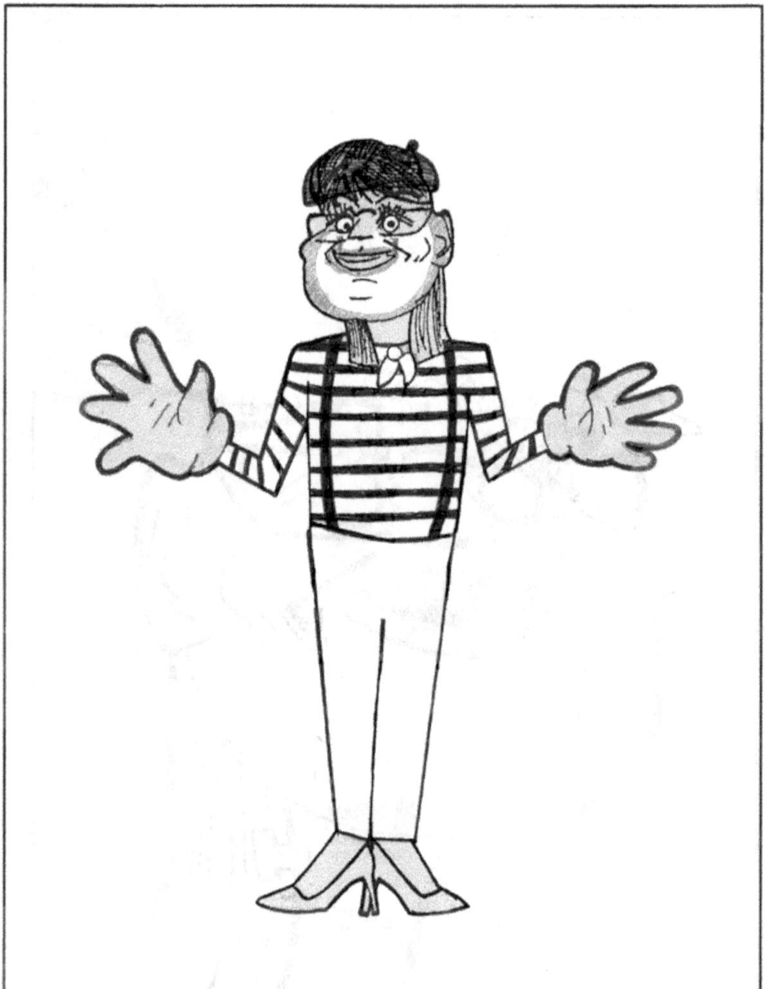

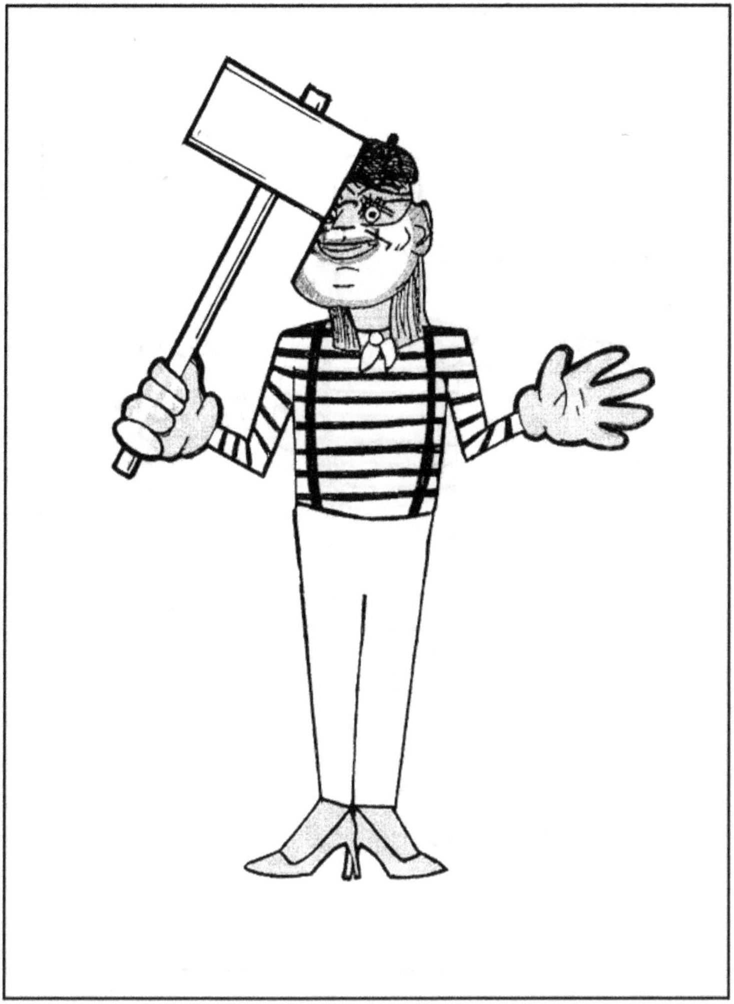

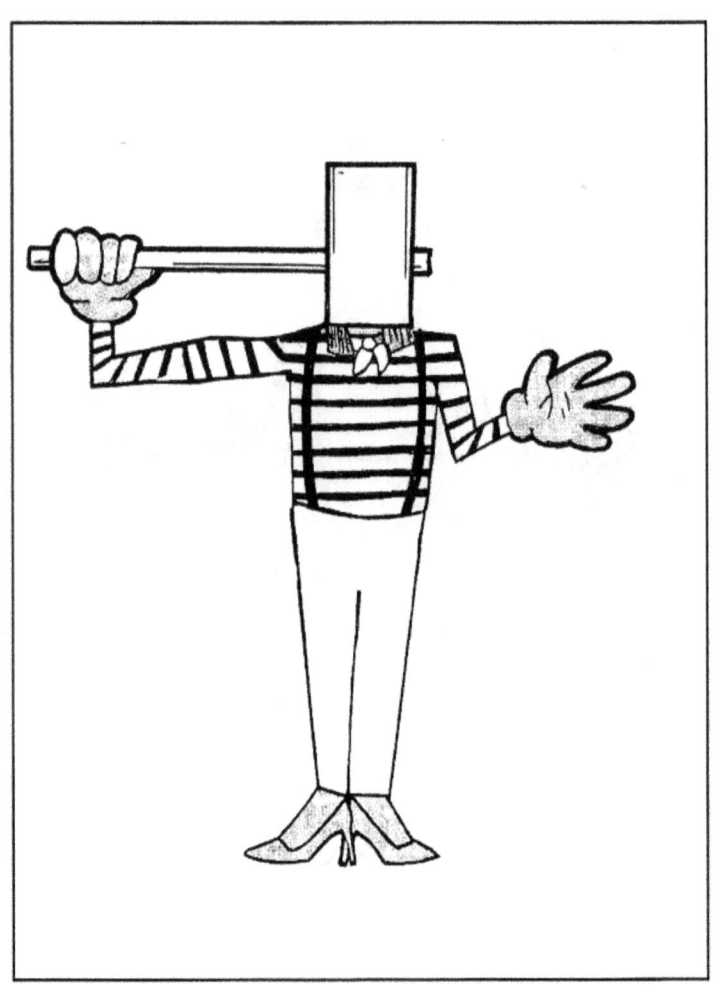

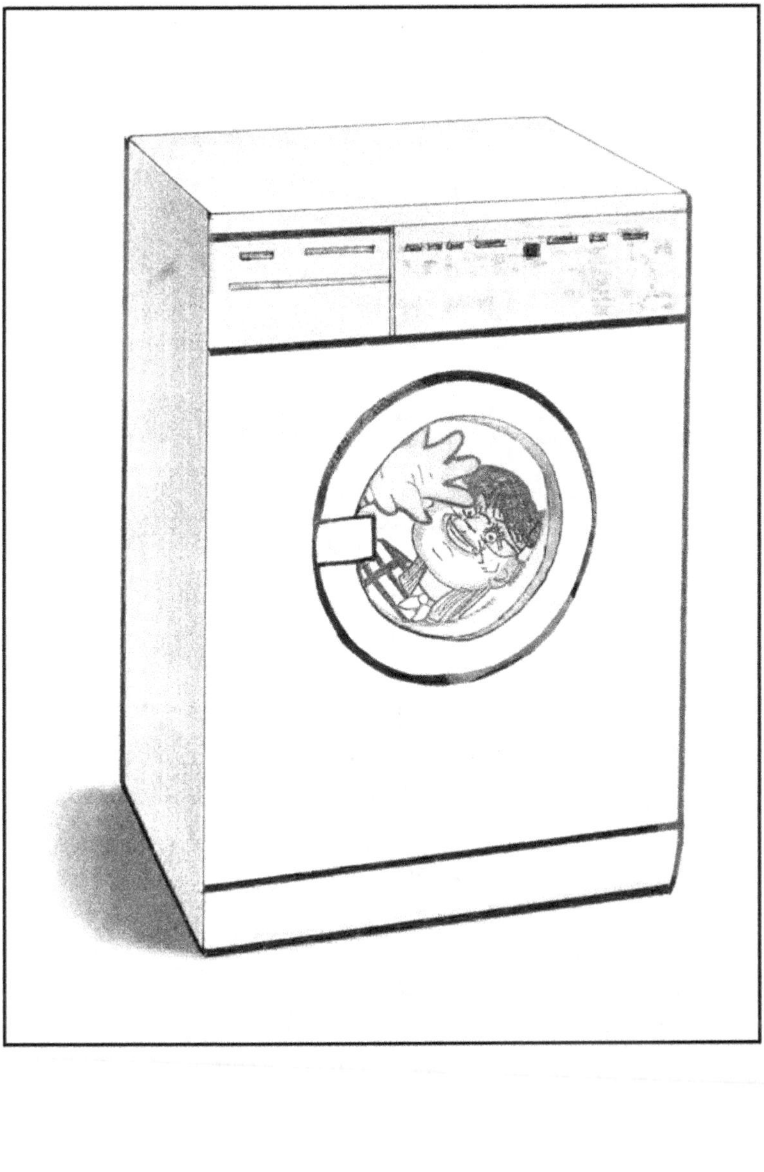

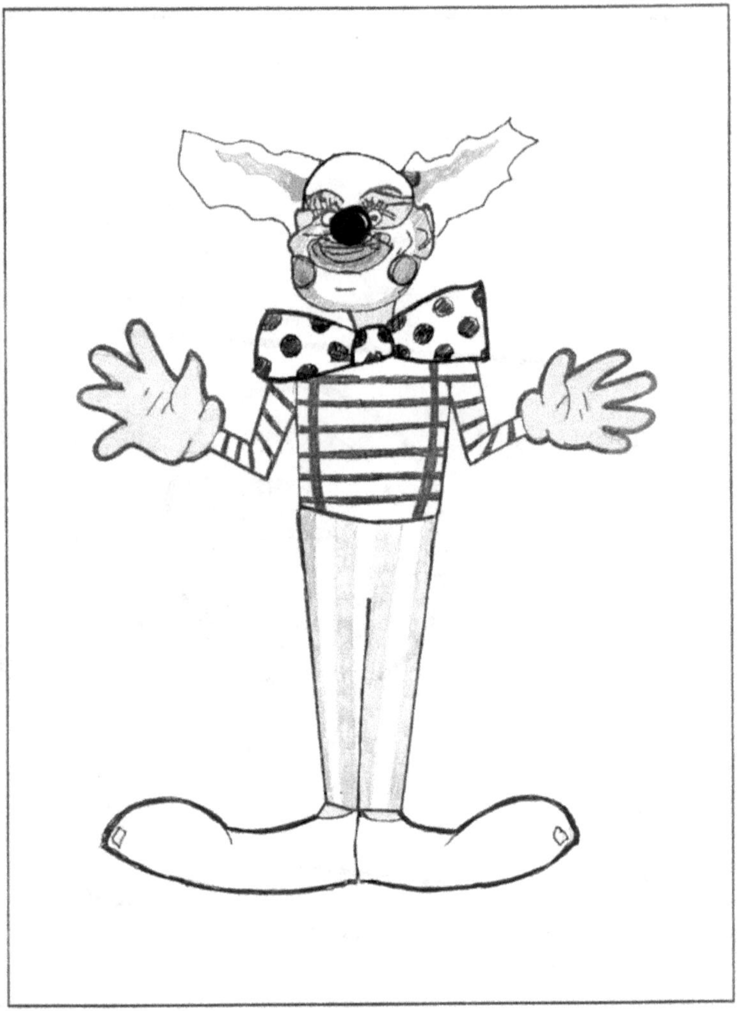

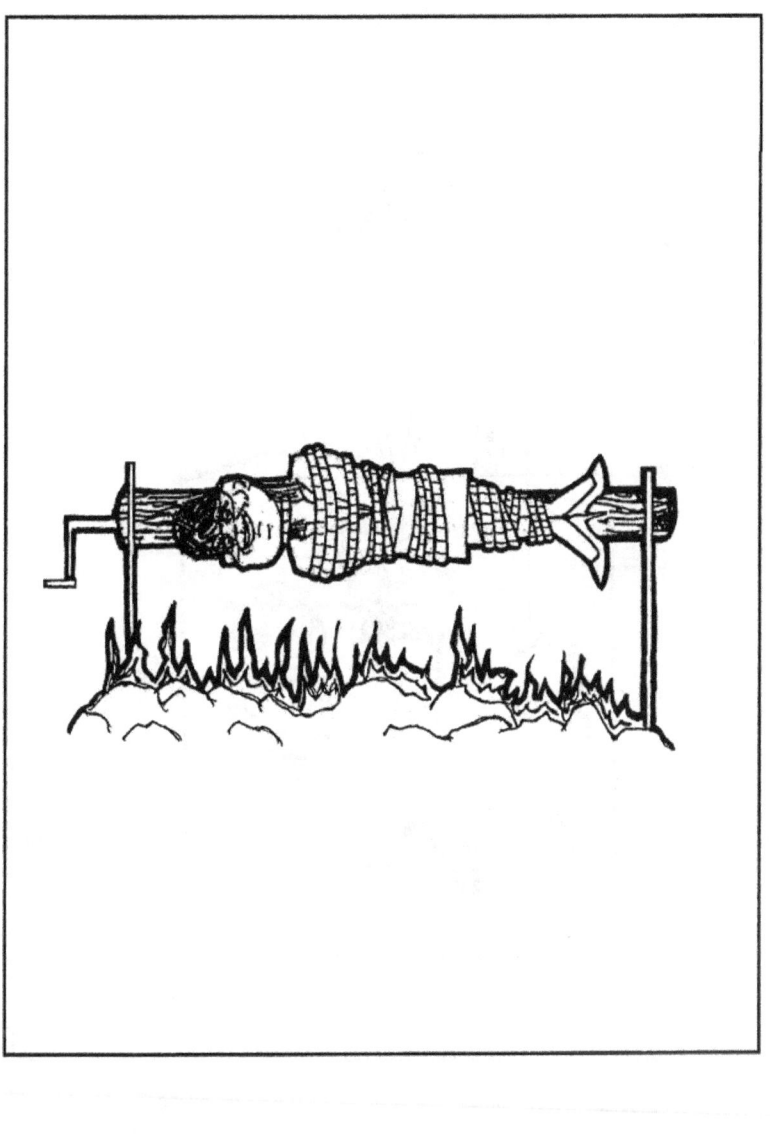

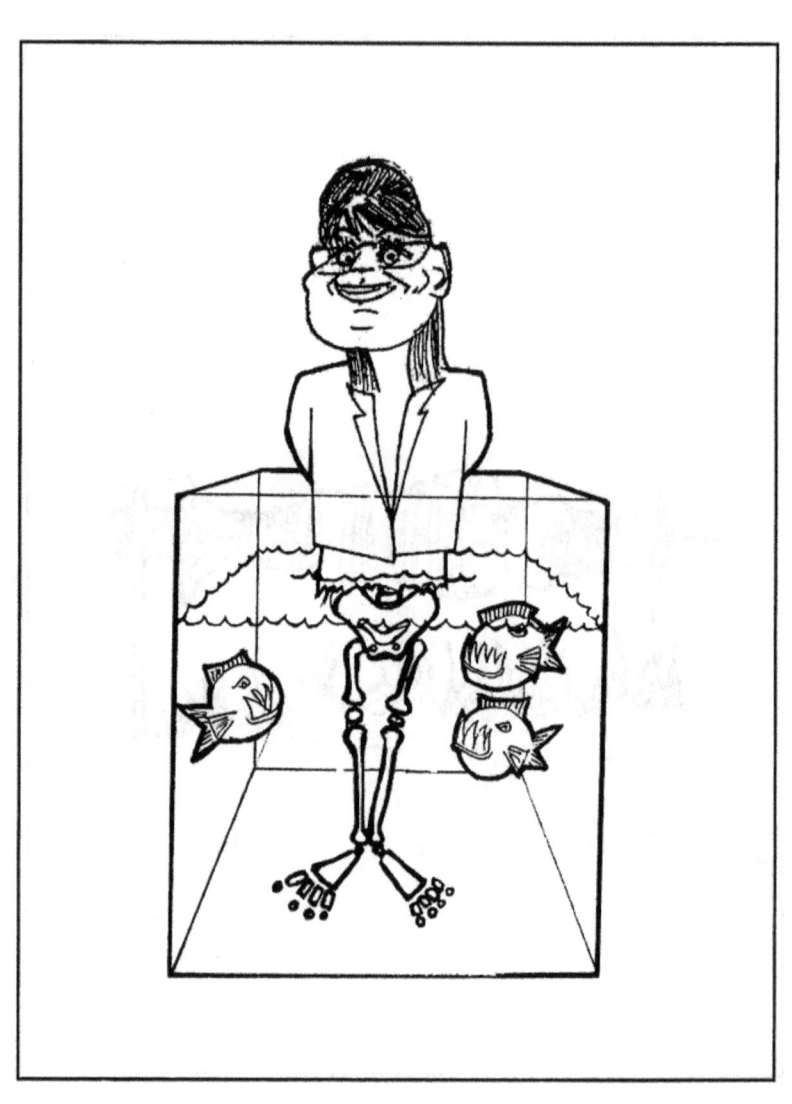

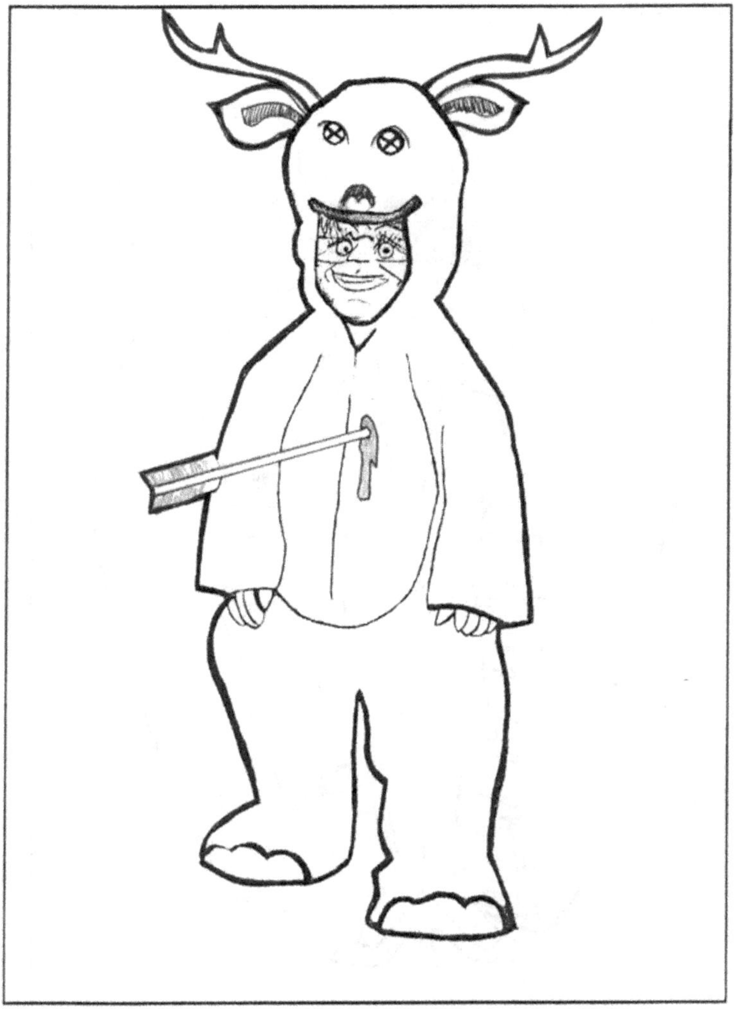

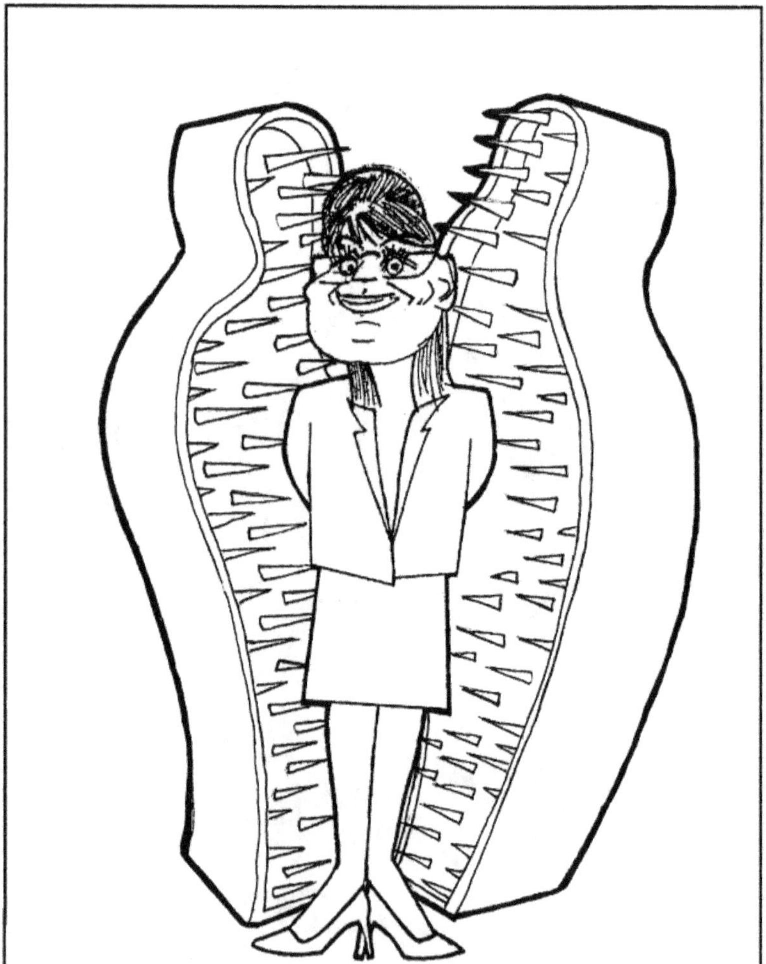

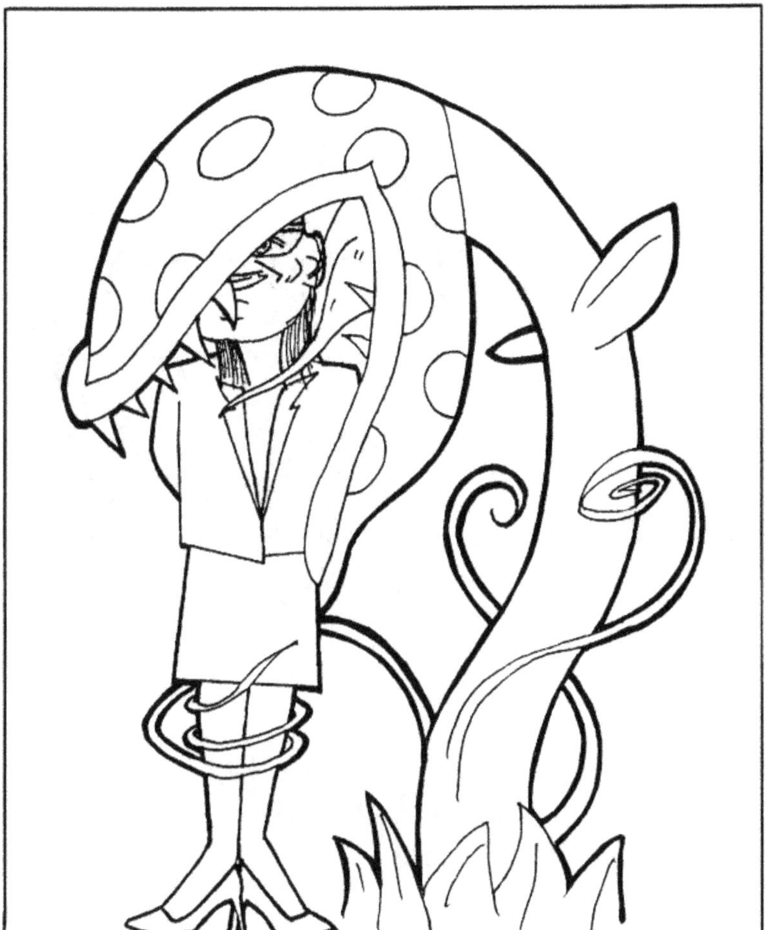

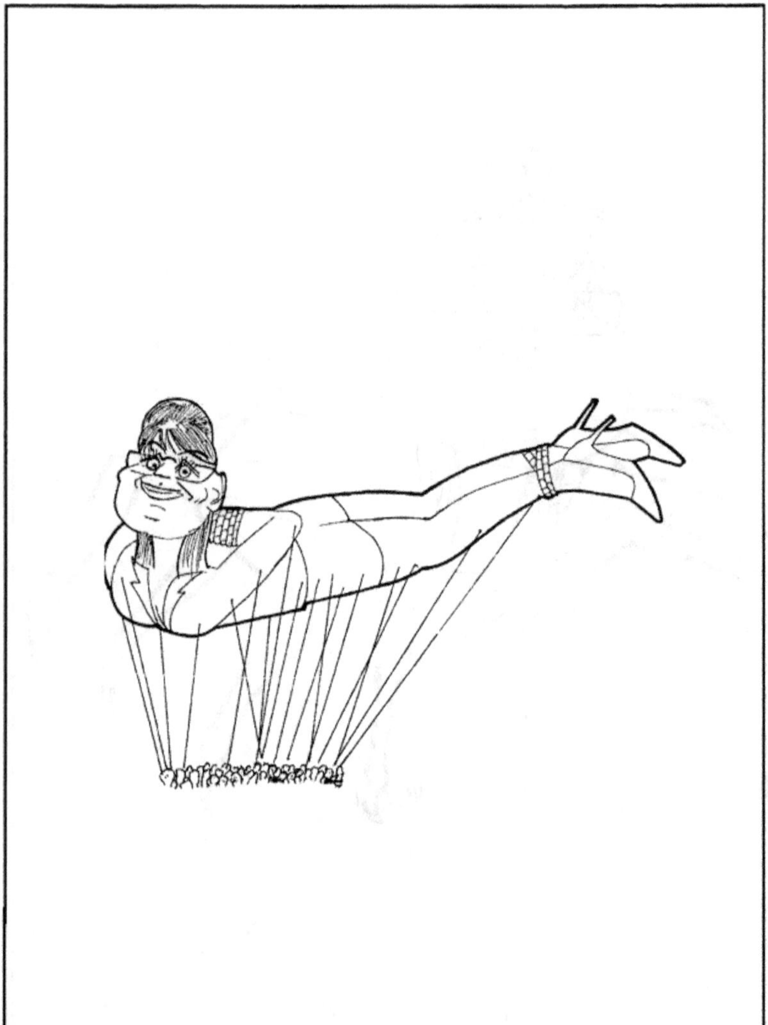

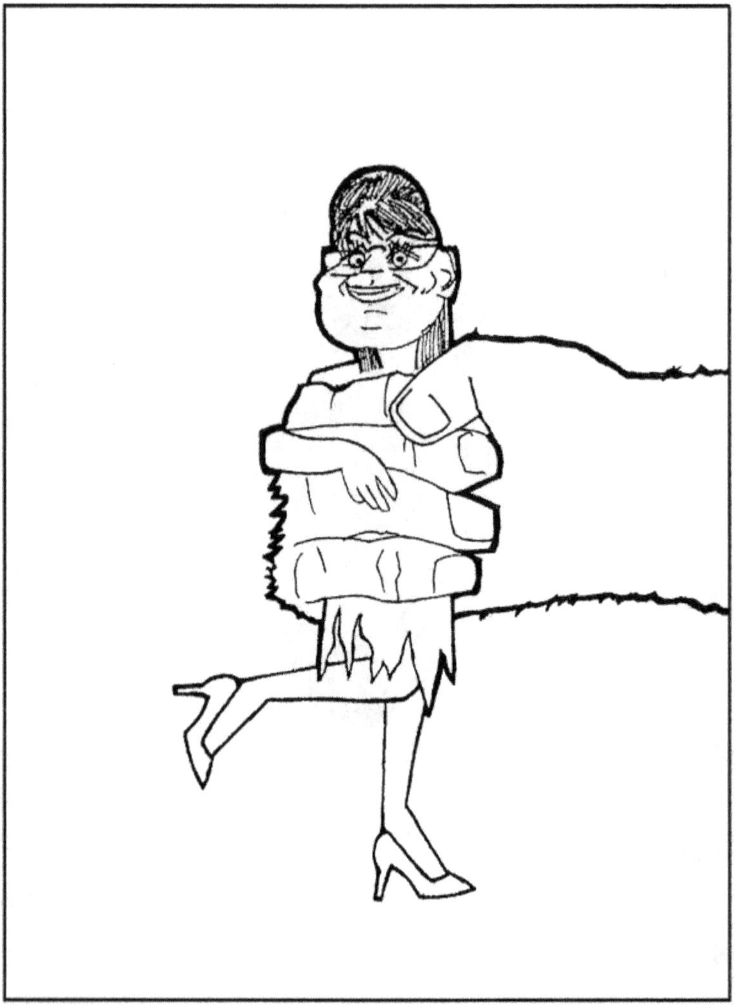

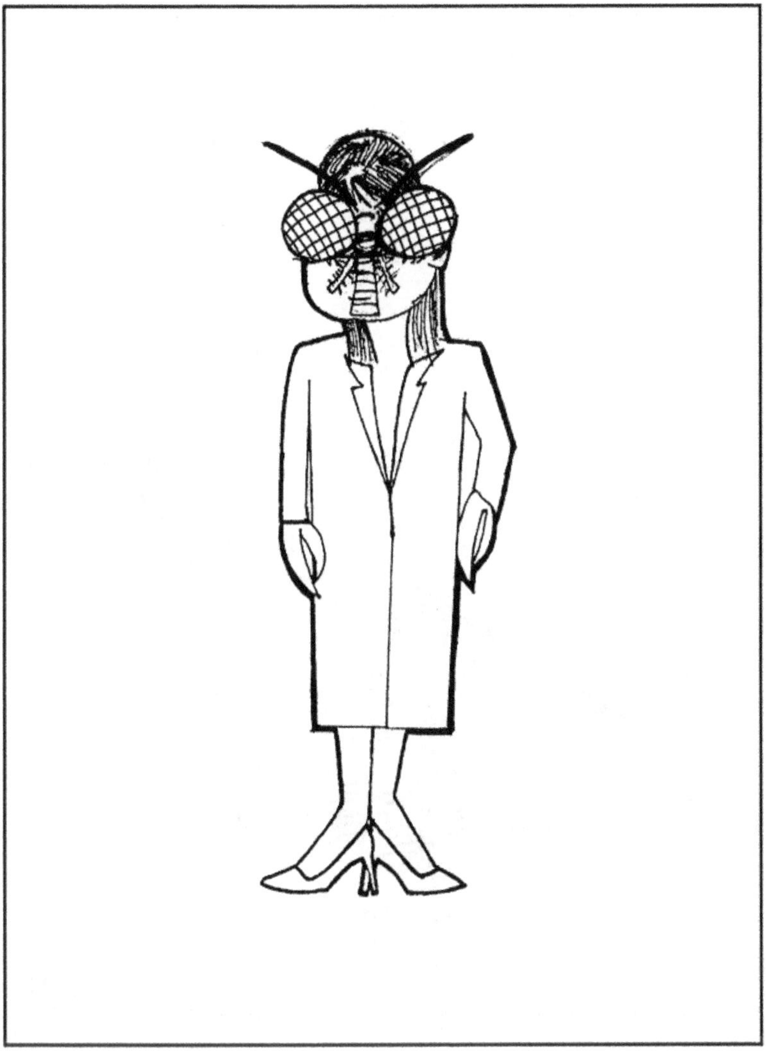

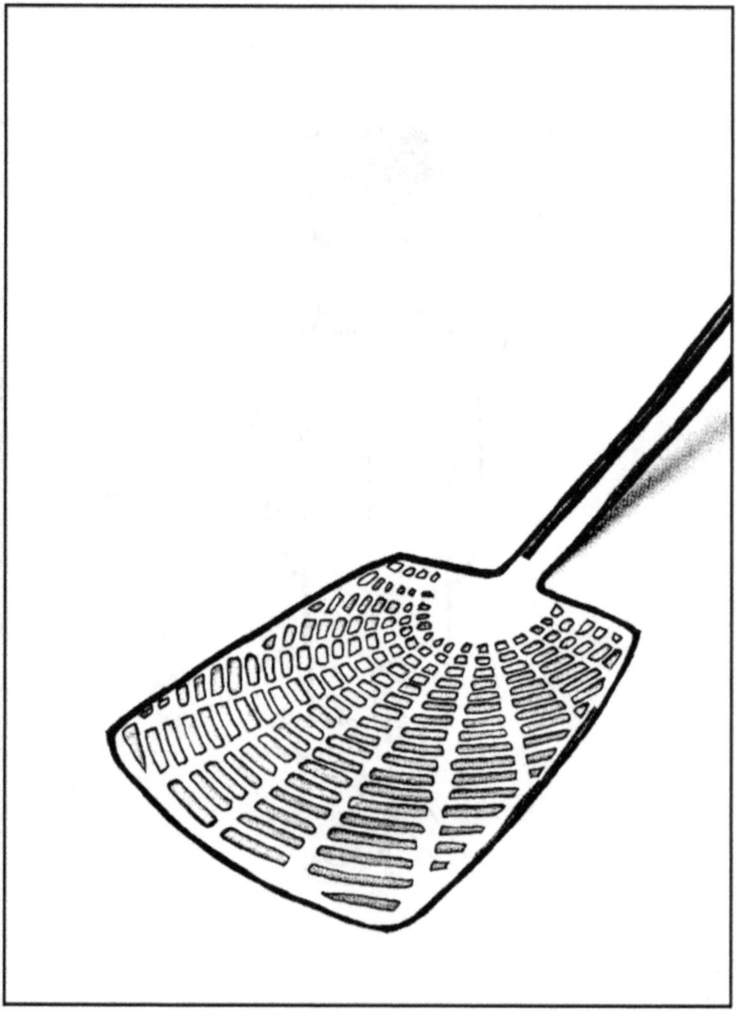

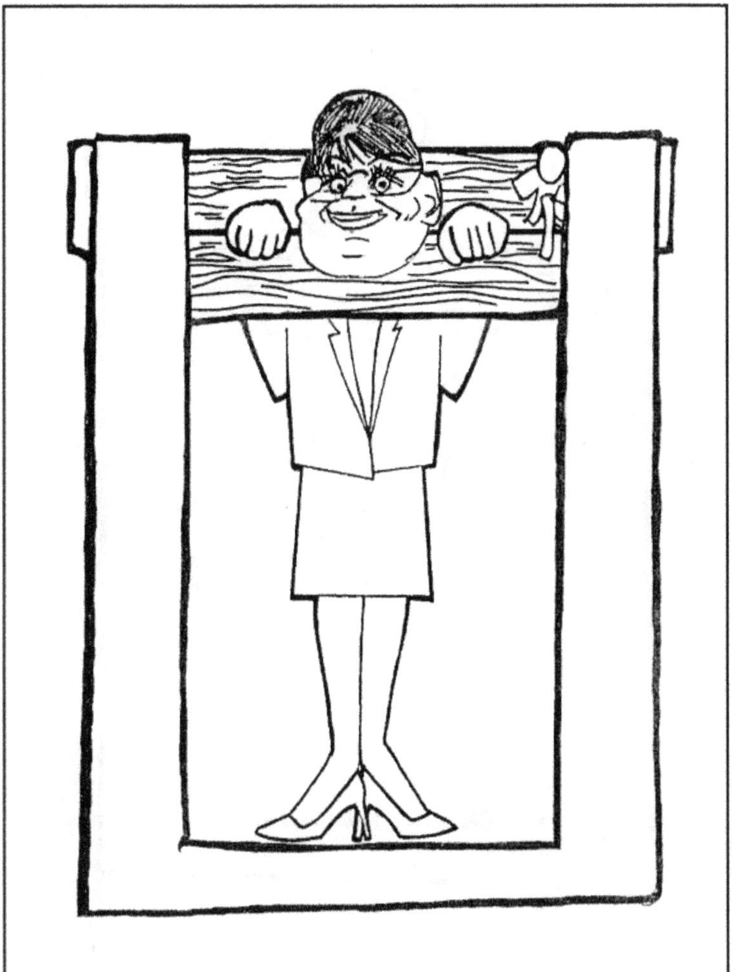

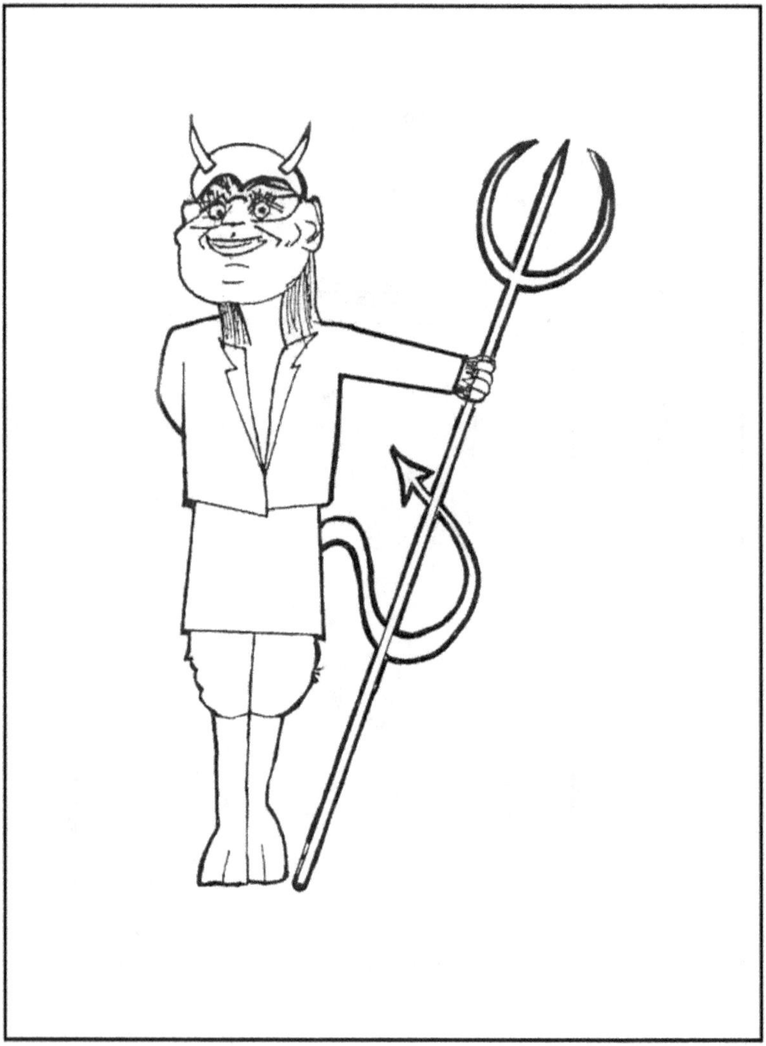

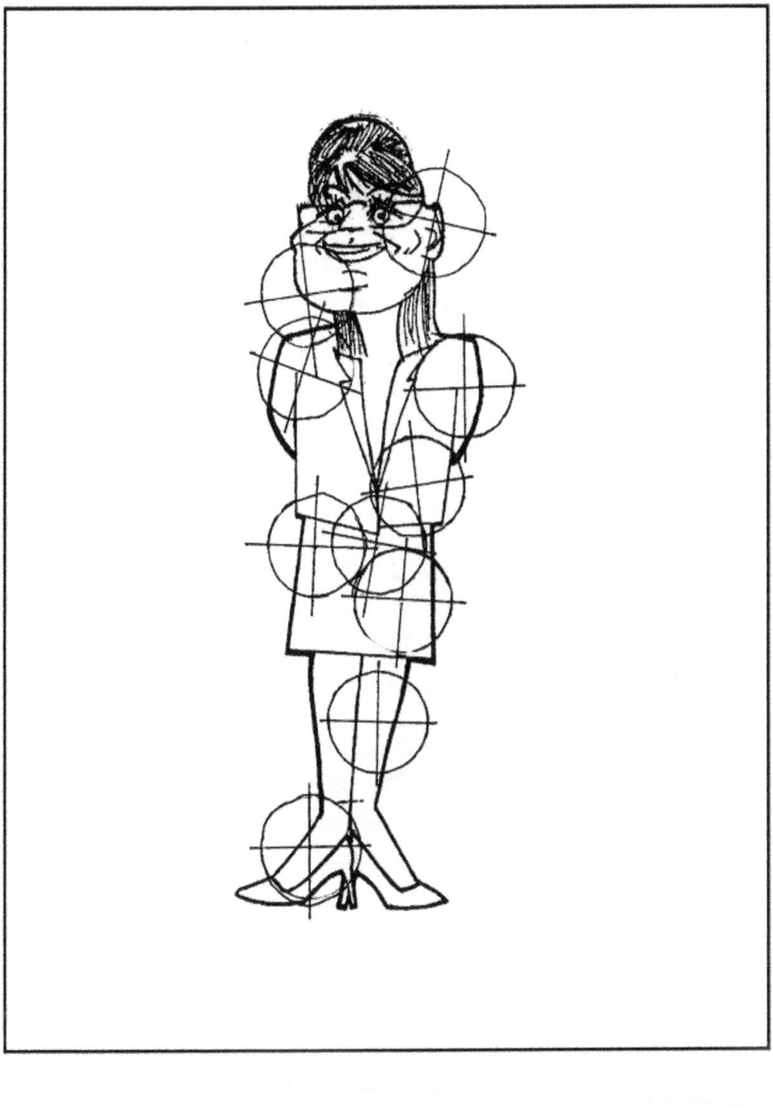

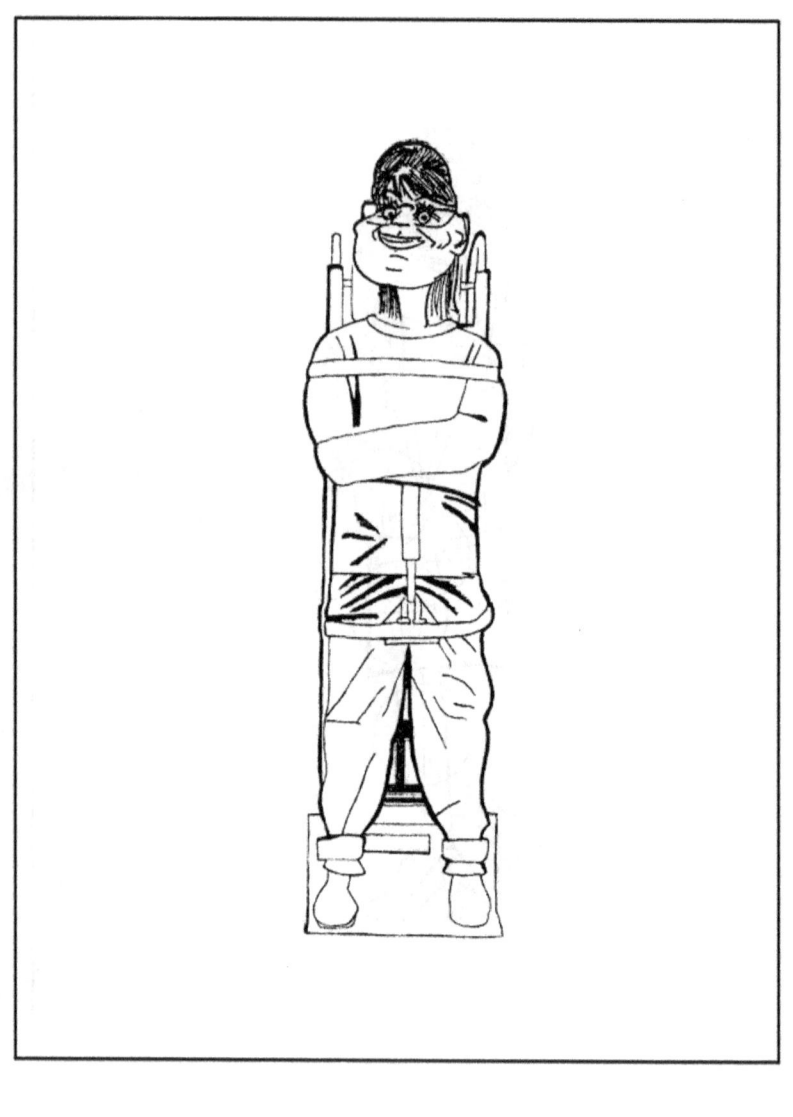

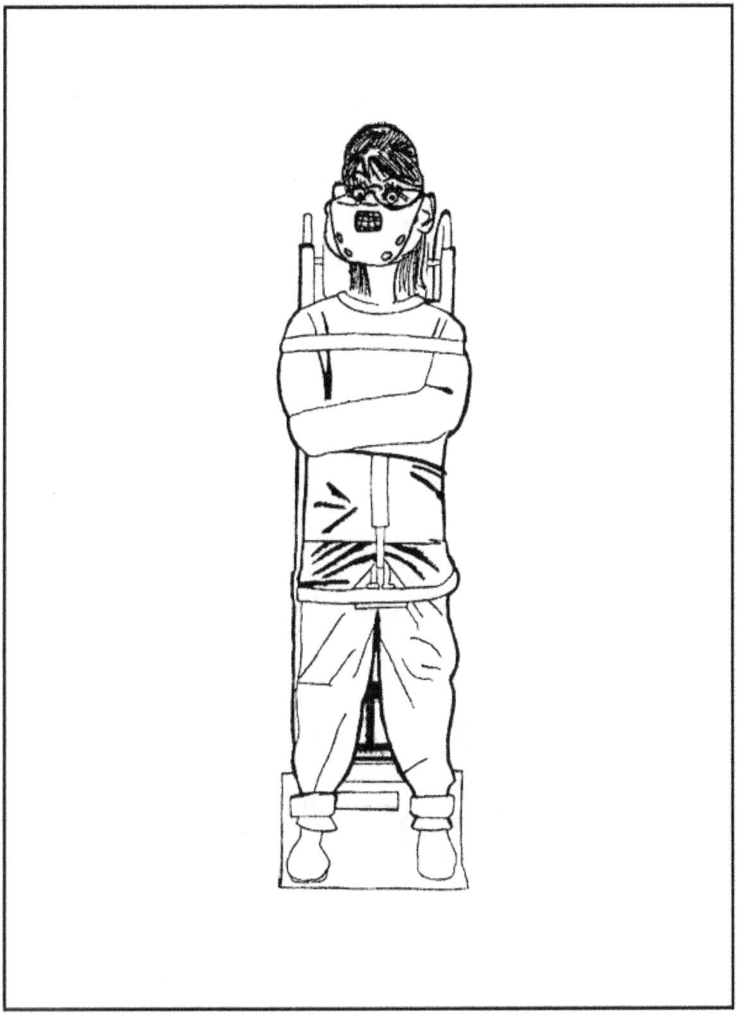

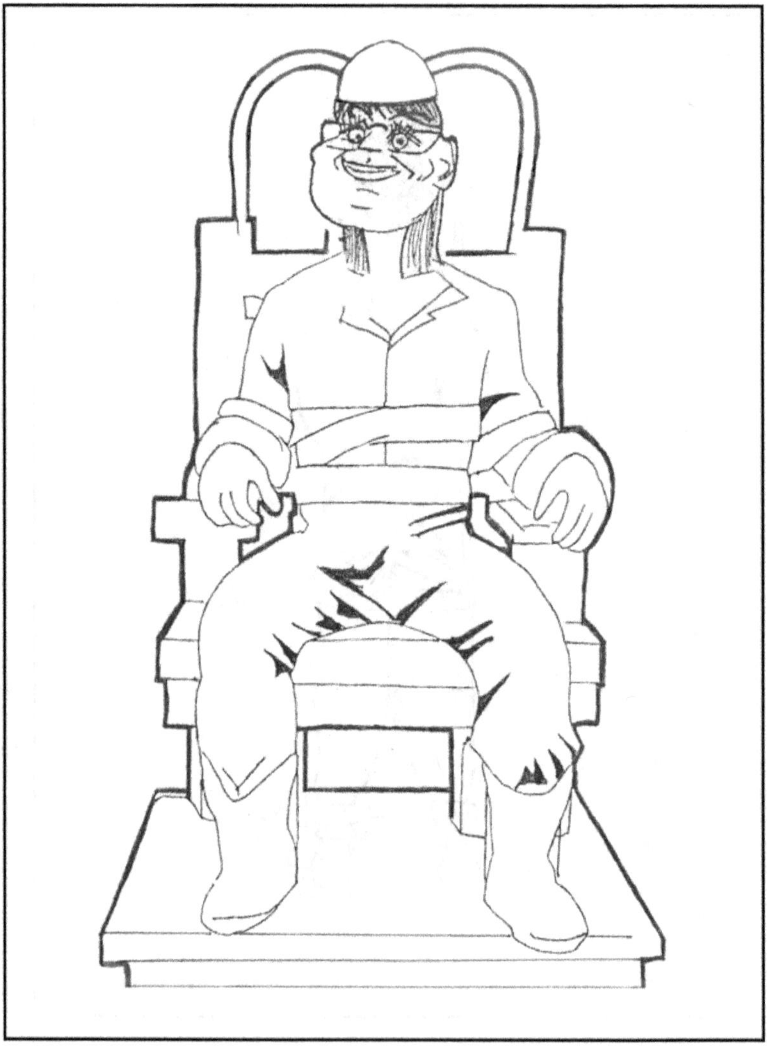

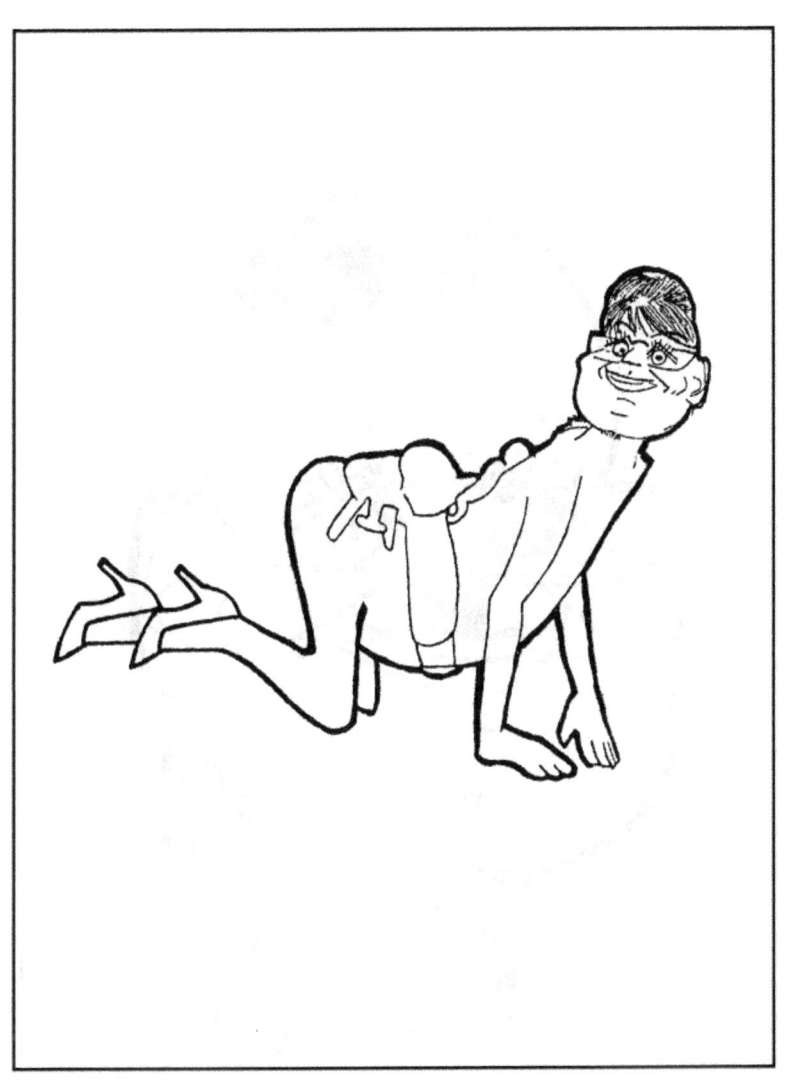

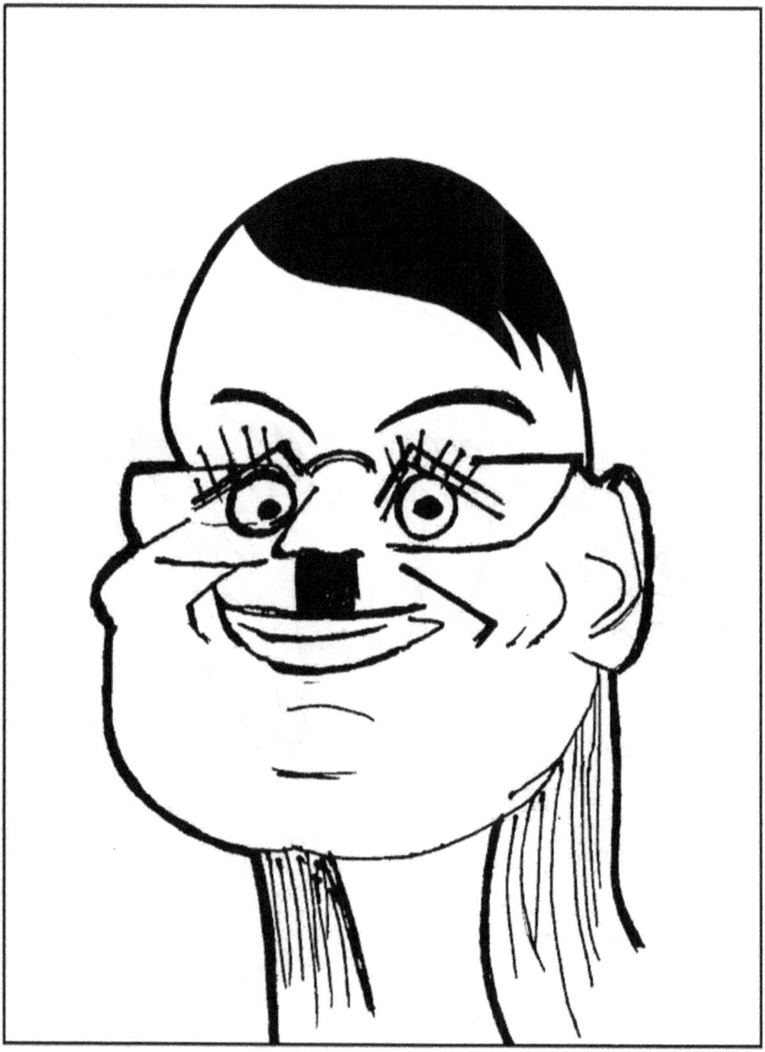

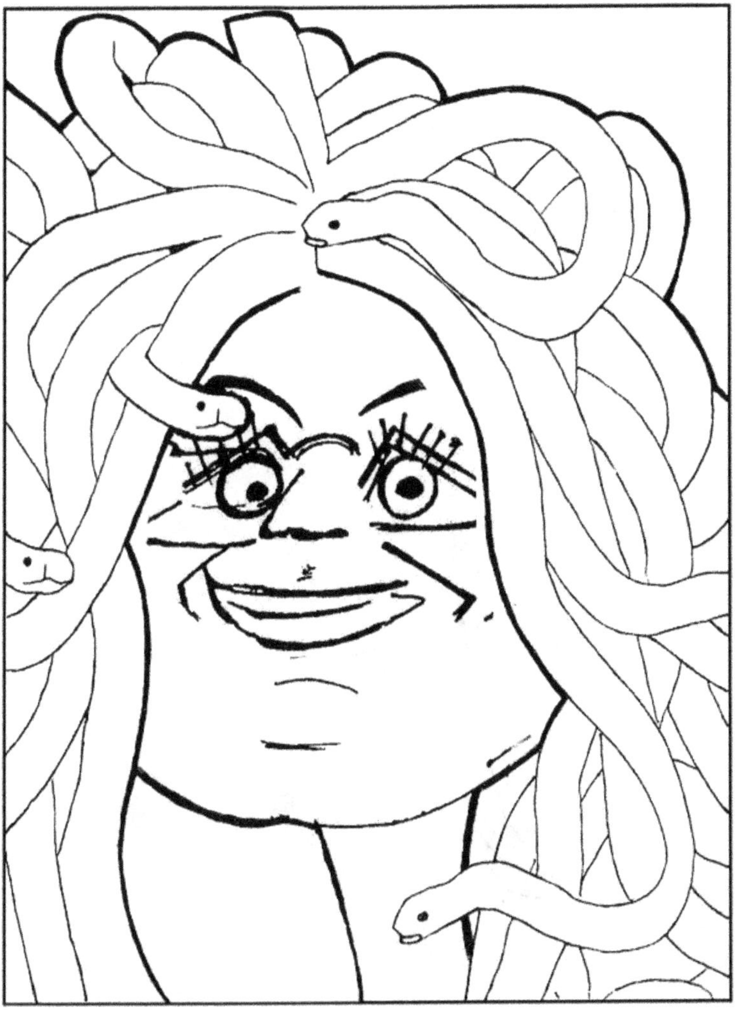

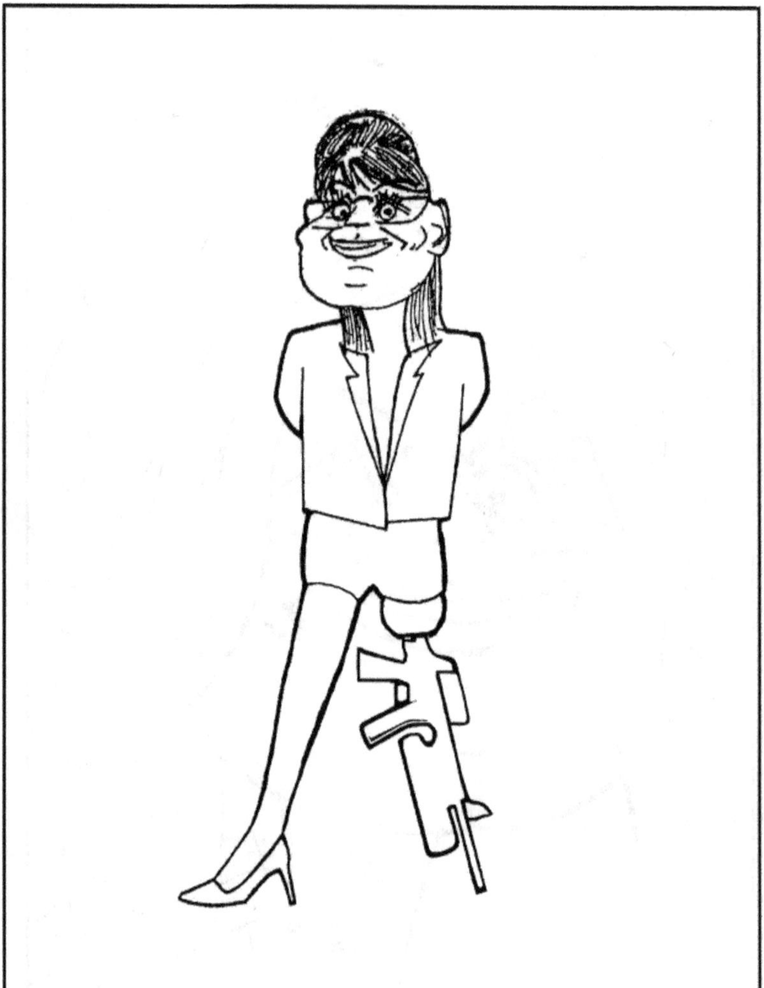

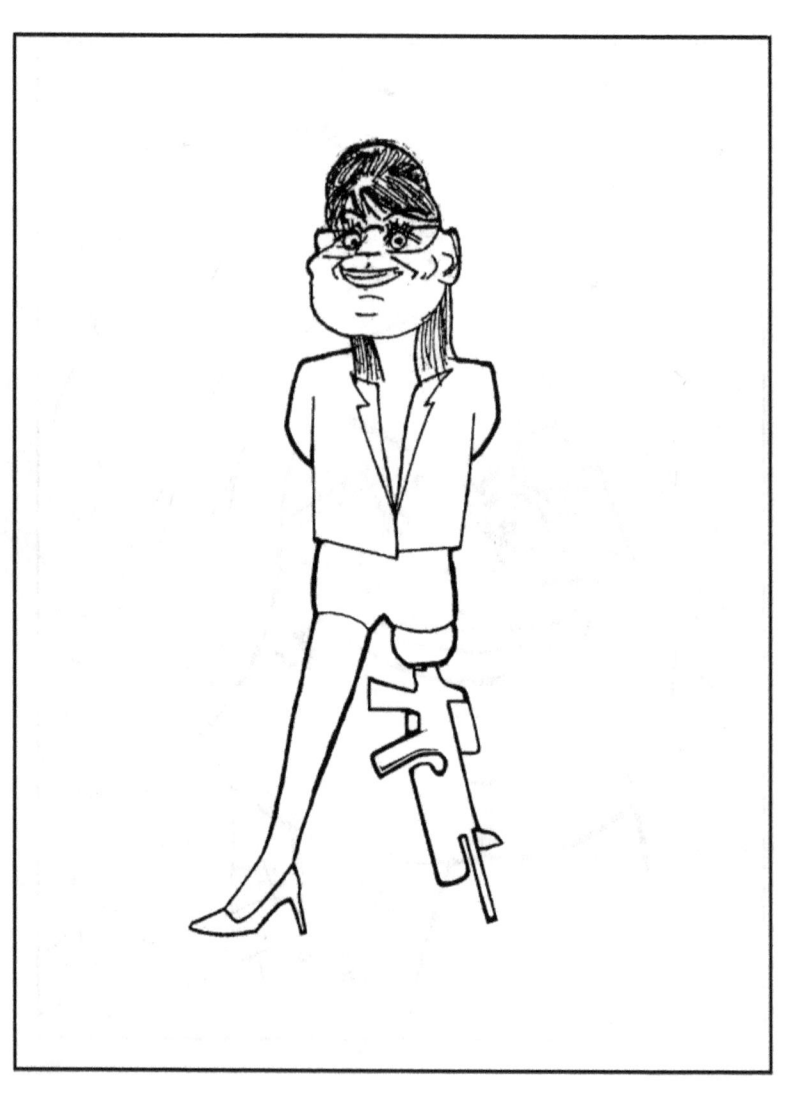

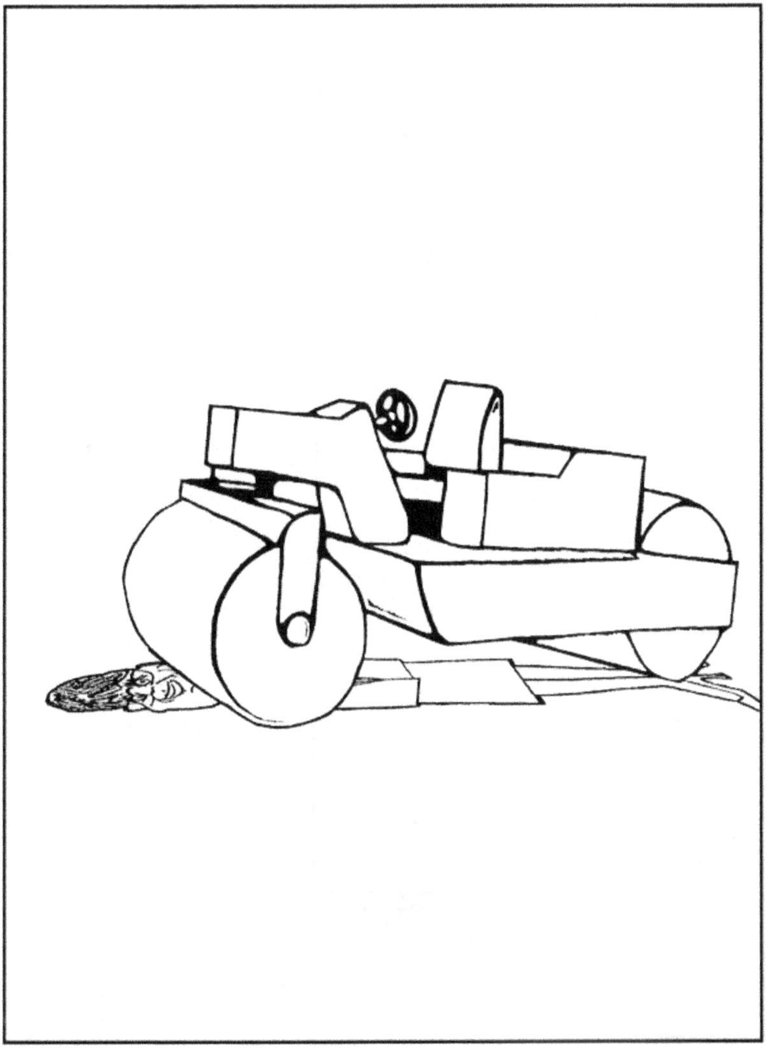

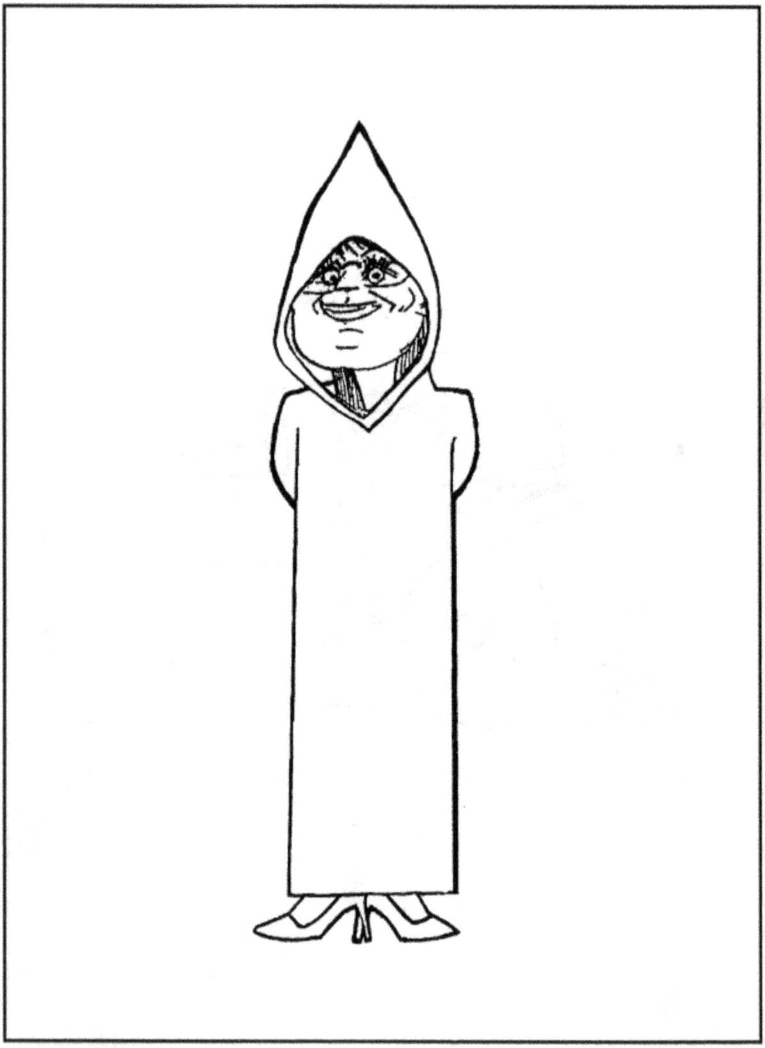

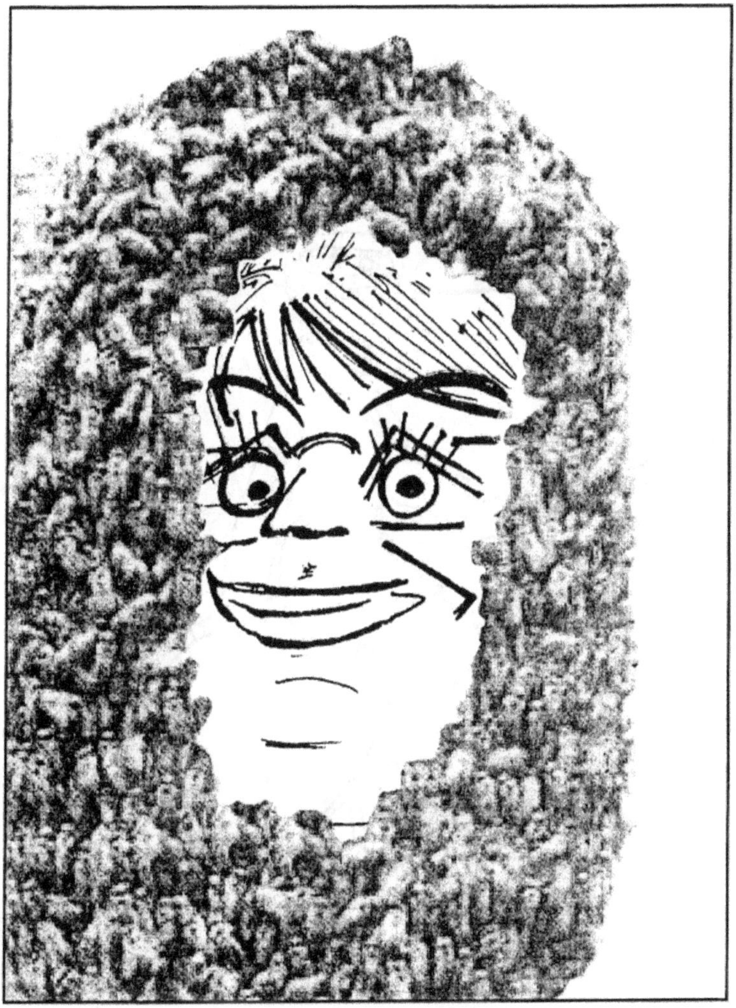

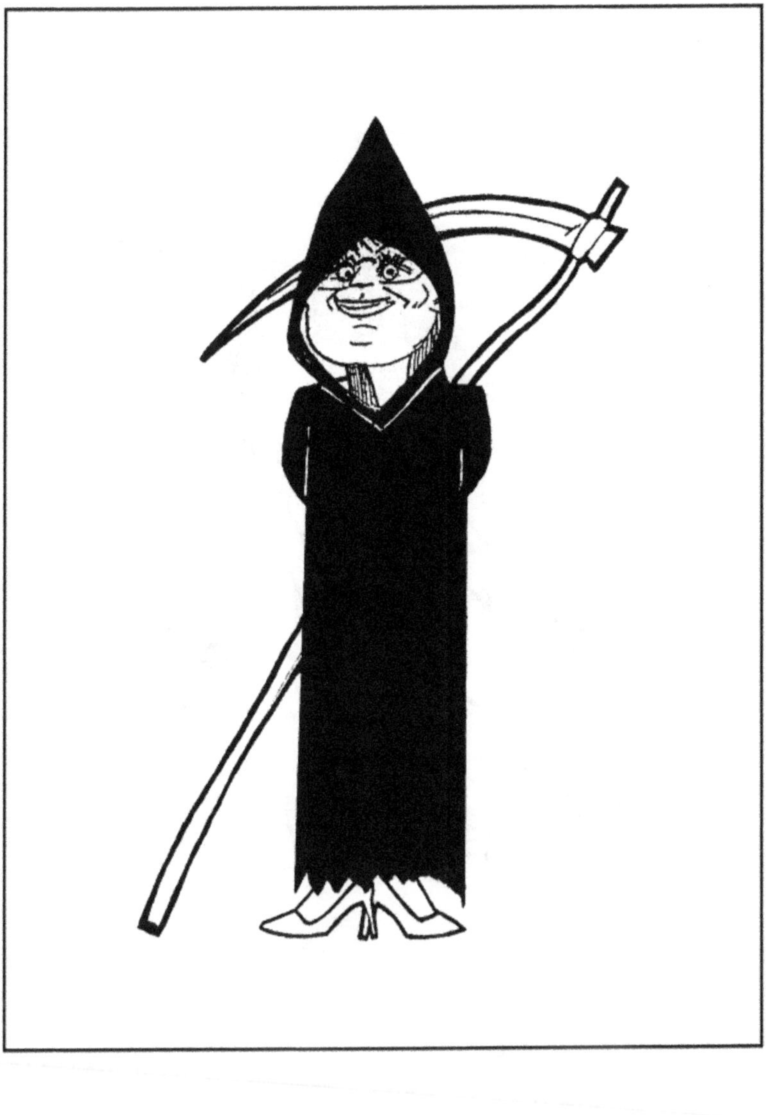

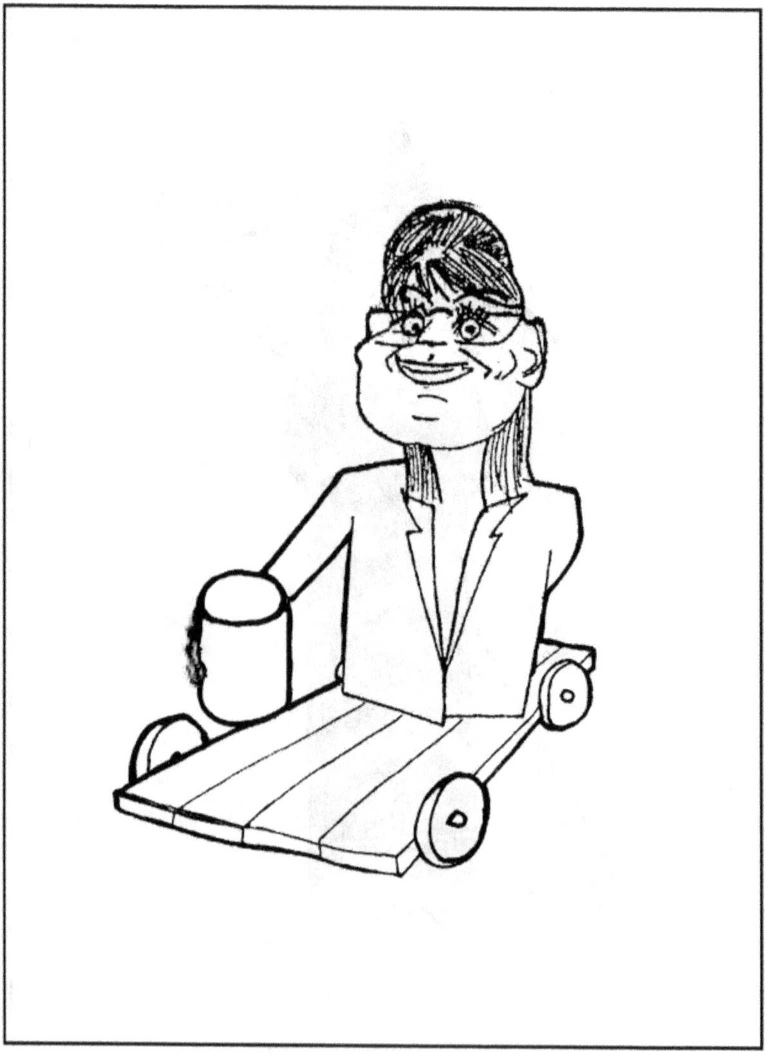

www.ingramcontent.com/pod-product-compliance
Lightning Source LLC
Chambersburg PA
CBHW071504070426
42452CB00041B/2288